D1459919

THE WAR ON WOMEN FROM "THE ROOT" TO "THE FRUIT!"

Which side are you on?

KEVIN MCGARY

The War on Women from "The Root" to "The Fruit!"
Edition 1.0 2020

Contact the author at: KevinMcGary@RationalFreePress.com

Published in Canada and the United States by
Rational Free Press

Other titles by this author:
JUST "Justly Justice"

ISBN
978-1-7772018-0-7

Contents

Preface

It is hard to fully express my gratitude and excitement about this, my fourth book. It is especially gratifying to have received much coaching, scholarship, and encouragement from so many that helped make this book possible. Based on early input, I am very excited about the reactions and outcomes this book will produce as it traverses from person-to-person.

While all my prior writings had significant social/cultural implications, none of my previous works captivated and moved me with new insight and with overwhelming love and compassion for humanity that this one has. That book was quite illuminating for me, and my whole perspective and ideology has been permanently altered. That said, I wrote out of an urgent sense of renewed impetus for dutiful encouragement and admonition about the war on women. This subject is inescapable and touches everyone (all of humanity) and therefore has far-reaching implications. Since it affects everyone, everyone should have a perspective, opinion, and personal stance about it.

With a tremendous amount of arcane rhetoric being spouted about almost any topic these days, this book is written to help reduce the rhetoric while "lifting the veil" on the truth. Having truth about the real (or perceived) war on women helps circumvent feelings of being misled and manipulated into believing in something that is assumed and/or false. In the end, my hope is this read is ingested and appropriately critiqued as it is overlaid anew onto personal ideologies and life journey.

I want to offer a special thanks to my aunt Karen McGary and the rest of my family for once again supporting and encouraging me through this process. Special thanks goes to Terry Barnes for the incredible cover art/ graphics and illustration as well! Additionally, many special friends including Larry Weins, Skip Vaccarello, Tom Rees, Kevin and Shondale Gray, Pastor Rob McCoy, Vincent Engobor, James Jenkins, Bill Federer, Kahn Holiday, Kolette Cole, Pastor Bryan Murphy, Lily Akopova, Julia Nelson, Wilson Farrar, Neil Mammen and so many more helped provide incredibly thoughtful and valuable feedback throughout this project. I offer big and unequivocal thanks to all!

Most importantly, this book is dedicated to My Father. If there are any good ideas, insights or perspectives in this book, He gets all the credit...I am eternally thankful and grateful that He takes such good care of me...

Thank You Father!

Introduction

In almost every domain, there are endless plausible claims of "wars" that are adversely affecting society and culture. Some include the war on the family, the war on men/boys (masculinity in general), the war on Religion/Christianity, the war on poverty/poor, the war on drugs, racial "wars" and countless others. This book is not written to exclude any of the many other viable "wars." It is written because there is one war that all the other "wars" emanate from (and/or are connected to). This war had been declared since the beginning of mankind, and due to its preeminence and pervasive impacts, it is the "mother of all wars" (literally and figuratively). Only one "war" aptly fits this description, and it's the "war on women."

Over the past twenty years, the "war on women" has become a "mainstream" socio/cultural talking point. While there are still many who may be unfamiliar with the distinctions "war on women," there are very many who live and "fight through it" it as an ever-present reality. It has now become an accepted mantra denoting gender inequality issues, "glass ceiling" in the workplace, women's empowerment initiatives (and etc.), and has reached a crescendo that now seems to intersect and overlay almost every area of grievance dominating interpersonal communication. Admittedly, when I would see articles of the war on women and listen to discussions about this war, it came across as the latest "cliché" and a part of socio/cultural nomenclature that rang hollow. I was left with, "How can 'the war on women' be taken seriously if it is just a fad used to bludgeon and put others on the defensive?" Well, through serious study and after taking a purposeful journey on the topic, I now know different! I have been provided a rather divine impartation on this issue, and now it has been evolved from being viewed as purely transient and metaphorical to becoming real, practical, and prescient.

Unveiling and providing additional revelation on a subject like the "war on women" is indeed lofty, but since it is now a "mainstream" mantra, it is past due. Due to its pervasive size and scope pervading every area and domain of culture, and every society in every region on earth, it is a necessary "reveal" for such a time as this! The "war on women" will be finally and dutifully unveiled in this book, and it's surely a "rocky ride," so govern your heart and "hold on to your seat" accordingly!

Prior to being given a deeper insight and revelation on the subject of the war on women, most often, I simply dismissed it as a metaphorical ruse. Other times, I dismissed it because feeling "if there were a true war on women, nothing can or will be done about it." As a man and often object of the hostility coming from those who self-describe as warriors fighting for women's rights, I felt powerless to intervene in any meaningful way. I only recently realized that irrespective of preconceived notions, this war is not trivial or imagined. There have been hundreds of millions who have been hurt and directly impacted by the plight of women and their respective standing. When we consider the sheer magnitude of the crush of humanity that has endured countless ways of being hurt, maligned, and have suffered wholly destructive indignities because they happen to be of a certain gender (in this case, female), it is irresponsible and wholly insensitive to shirk the fact that we are all vested in participating in ANY war that is so destructively impactful.

Our history and progeny depend on us, to tell the truth, stand for truth and correct wrongs (as best we can) as we pursue righteous causes and justice! We seem to be living through a historical period when socio/cultural paradigms escalate into aggressively emotional movements; this is a period when truth and justice are supremely important, as they help forestall social disintegration and active undermining of cherished alliances and institutions. That said, it's quite appropriate to ponder what are truly the righteous and just causes when it comes to the frequent refrain, industry, and nomenclature asserting the "war on women."

If we are sincere in our quest to help women become the powerful, thoughtful, compassionate, powerhouses God created them to be, we have to commit to serious introspection, even to the depths of our soul. While I have no doubt many thoughtful works have been produced and many scholars have attempted to address the war on women, the fact remains, women continue to be maligned, abused and enslaved more today (at disproportionally higher rates and in ever-increasing numbers) than at any time in the history of the world. This begs the question, "why?" Hundreds of years of persistent concerted efforts in empowering women's movements worldwide, yet very little has changed. What have we missed? Are there other elements and calculus that have yet to be factored into the women's rights and empowerment equation that we have yet to consider?

This book asserts that there are indeed other dynamics, elements, and equations that have tremendously negatively impacted the peril of women, and their current plight is the most significant confirmation. Tactics and strategies have been designed to help via the analogy of the "war" and battlefield, and yet no cohesive, effective battlefield actions have ensued. With the assertion that the war is real, this book confirms that one of the biggest impediments to success is the fact that the battle (war on women) has been waged and is feverishly raging, but it has not been consistently understood; therefore, limited knowledge of the precepts of war and how it is to be waged, has limited effective strategies on the battlefield. This book is designed to help provide all combatants with what's needed to fully understand the war and its roots in order to wage war and combat on behalf of all women effectively.

A new understanding and vision for what is truly at stake in the war on women have been revolutionary thinking for me; no doubt, you will be greatly challenged as well! Again, I believe the biggest challenge will come from your very soul. The soul is where "mind," "will," and "emotions" reside, and as you read from chapter to chapter, places in the realm of the soul will morph and change (if you allow them) into a more determined and committed place of resolve. To this end, the chapters of this book are designed to include "opening statements" at the beginning of chapters, and "closing arguments" at the end. The verbiage of the courts is used in this regard because in actual court trials, someone has been arrested and accused, and arguments ensue about guilt or innocence. I liken this to the condition of our souls. Because this reading will challenge at the level of the soul, I use the metaphor of our very souls having been "arrested" (wittingly or unwittingly), and is now on trial. Arguments will be presented with hopes of setting it free via facts and truth. Utilizing opening and closing arguments appropriately allows for introspection and circumspection as we transcend existing preconceived notions and mindsets and move to new levels of enlightenment and understanding.

Lastly, you will see that the war on women culminates in a crescendo of chaos that ultimately touches every arena and domain of our lives. You will see maladies emerging from basic human ontology, a core ideology, religion, social movements, and evolving socio/cultural norms that undergird the fundamentals and premise of the "war on women!" This is a fascinating part of the journey, and I pray your personal commitment and sincerity in helping turn the tide in the "war on women" encourages a dogged pursuit of truth and justice. While this book will clarify and confirm facts about the war on women that have yet to be widely considered nor largely pursued, it is not intended to be the exhaustive "end-all" "be-all," so there is much room for additional study and understanding. Ultimately, changes in the realm of the soul are usually not immediate; therefore, "recursive iteration" (redundancy) is used to make sure the "dots are being connected" and change in perceptions are indeed being considered.

Are you ready for the unveiling and "big reveal?" Godspeed as you embark on this profound journey of the soul!

PART I
THE ROOT

Unveiling The Root And Premise Of The War

CHAPTER 1

JOURNEY TO THE BATTLE

Opening Statement:

There is a battle! The battle has been raging for millennia, but until recently, it has been clouded and shrouded. Based on disproportional negative outcomes however, it is now becoming clear, the target of the battle is women! Generally speaking, women have been targeted, maligned, and undermined more than men, and now it's time we discover why! A journey to the battlefield provides appropriate time to get hearts and mind aligned and prepared for war, while also overviewing of the scope of the battle. This helps better prepare combatants for what's to come.

Whether you currently view the war on women with skepticism, or you actually live it as an ever-present reality, just the threat of a war against women implies precaution and preparation. With any battle, soldiers must prepare by demonstrating a mindset and determination for destroying enemy/forces, bring adequate battle supplies for the respective battlefield landscape, confirm understanding of rules conditions of engagement, and a working knowledge of the enemy and associated tactics and strategies. These are the basic necessities for the battlefield. After dutiful confirmation of preparedness, soldiers begin to make the trek to the battlefield. The aforementioned basic battle preparations are necessary for any war, and precautionary preparation to engage in the battle in the war on women is no different! The only impediment, however, is the enemy of women may not be obvious; perhaps he's veiled and concealed. This means, in order to confirm an actual purposeful affront against women, an effort must be made to reveal a foe.

Reliance on rhetoric, hyperbole and base symbolism of current social/cultural affronts to women to reveal a foe is not reliable and accurately determinative. A more reliable source for uncovering a plausible foe emerges with a simple deconstruction of events starting from the beginning of humankind. That said, Adam & Eve are the ideal start-point; a Biblical account of events and respective trajectory would affirm historical accuracy of humankind and a reliable source to account for a foe.

From Biblical accounts, Adam and Eve seem to have loved and adored one another as equal. As a matter of fact, it almost seems that Eve felt quite comfortable acting as an independent thinker and possessing just as much (or more) persuasion and influence as Adam. Based on Adam's actions toward acceptance and acquiescence to Eve's demands to indulge in her newfound "fruit," he certainly seemed to have honored and respected her as equal (even as he knew full- well his actions would undermine his relationship with God). That being said, what happened since that time? When was the pivot that turned woman from being an "equal" while in the Garden of Eden, into being unequal and a target for some of the worst atrocities ever since? The answer is, there was a diabolical foe that emerged.

Biblical history will confirm there is an actual foe in the war on women. The unveiling of an actual war on women, a foe, and confirmation of the battleground will force a fundamental challenge to everyone's personal worldview! When we begin to see "the war" and the merit and recriminations therein, the world and the lens/prism through which we perceive it will be challenged; the most significant challenge will come in the arena of a personal worldview. Personal worldviews are inescapable, and they drive our individual narratives that create zeal and determination while moving us into action (or inaction). Modern-day theologian, Dr. Ravi Zacharias, in his profound studies and writings, consistently confirms that "everyone has a worldview." "A worldview basically offers answers to four necessary questions: Origin, Meaning, Morality, and Destiny. He then confirms… "all answers put together (in relation to origin, meaning, morality, and destiny) must be coherent." That said, the quest of this journey is to help "connect the dots," culminating in overarching "answers" to the *origin of life, the meaning of life*, the *morality of life*, and how "the war on women" has a profound impact on everyone's *eternal destiny*. The coherency of ensuing revelations will precipitate a change in personal worldview. The new worldview will change individual actions and intentions that can ultimately lead to positive cultural shifts in the "war on women" battle.

While this subject matter will (at least on the surface) cause us to want to storm the battlefield on behalf of women, this journey to the gates of discovery is not for the faint of heart. It is an actual challenge to all. Again, it is designed to challenge existing thoughts, ideas, and perspectives on what you think are already known about women. It will change thoughts of what we think we already know about the "war on women." And it will challenge how we assume "the war" began. It will challenge thoughts about nature and humanity. And, it will challenge thinking about God and the respective realms and paradigms of "good vs. evil!" In short, this journey is vitally important to the extent it is destined to challenge at the core of the soul, and force you to know things you may wish (in the end) that you would not have learned. Author Alice Hoffman is quoted as saying, "once you know some things, you can't unknow them. It's a burden that can never be given away." For participants in this journey to the battlefield of the war on women, there are no truer words! I pray there will be an incessant burning burden that will overtake you as an epiphany travels to the deepest crevices of the soul and forces new thinking and actions toward the real and quite tangible war on women!

Let's sojourn together in a fascinating real-life adventure that helps us really understand the foundational launch points, battle lines & progressions, and historical pivots of "the war on women from the root to the fruit!"

Closing Argument:

There are a real war and battle. The battlefield forces have prepared and are in place. While we perceive the target is women, the foe must be identified so the battle can ensue on their behalf. This war has significant cosmic repercussions that can only be overcome as we begin to observe and perceive it, then commit to fighting on the right side of it. To succeed in warring for women, we will journey to the front line of the war on the respective battlefield. After recognizing what's at stake in this war, all will be challenged in the realm of the soul, and a permanent change to collective mindsets will ensue.

CHAPTER 2

BATTLEFIELD WOMEN: ROOT OF "THE WAR"

Opening Statement:

Facts about history will confirm we are born into a preexisting war. It is an existential war. The war is not our fault, as it predates us. We are automatically enlisted into the battle. Our fundamental role is to be a soldier on one side vs. the other. There is no "safe space," neutral or middle ground! It's a binary war, meaning there are only two sides; everyone (without prejudice) is enlisted as a soldier combatant and forced to choose one side or the other. It's a declared war on women! The question that must be thoroughly considered is, "On which side are you fighting?"

At this juncture, there may be a struggle with wrapping your mind around the idea there may be an actually declared war on women, and an actual foe waging war. That said, to prevent any misinterpretation or misrepresentation, accurately defining the term "war" becomes paramount. War is a common term used in myriad contexts, but when asserting new ways to understand and perceive even terms used as part of common parlance, a precise definition is always the best practice. The Merriam-Webster dictionary defines war as: "open and declared hostile conflict"; "hostility, conflict." Most other dictionaries define war in the same way. That said, its safe to confirm that war can be characterized and distinguished by having hostile enemies involved in the conflict, participating in battles buttressed by enmity, and undergirded by hatred. The aforementioned definition provides rational clarity about war. When we overlay the actual definition of the war onto today's cultural/socio characterization and nomenclature of the war on women, we have to wonder where is the open and declared a hostile conflict, and when exactly did it occur? Furthermore, what is the root of this war?

In her writings in the late 1980s and 1990s, radical feminist Andrea Dworkin argued there was a war on women. As her writings took root, the "war on women" vernacular took root. As a slogan, the "war on women" became a normal and accepted distinction during the era of George W. Bush. During the Bush Presidency, many professed feminists asserted Republican Party policies restricted women's rights and actively prevented the advancement of women. In particular, they asserted that there was an explicit encouragement of workplace discrimination against women, a tacit acceptance of violence against women, and a restriction of "reproductive health" (abortion services) that unduly harmed women. Today, many women wholly support the contention that these affronts are systemic and culminate in an actual war on women!

At this point, serious consideration should be given to what has already been confirmed as the definition of war in juxtaposition to what is currently characterized and accepted as the "war on women." While President George W. Bush and the Republican Party certainly had their share of abhorrent "policy issues," and society/culture has certainly been fraught with systemic abuses and derelictions against women, realistically these affronts cannot be construed as the root causes for having a purposefully declared hostile, hate- laden, enmity-filled war against women.

The fact is, the "war on women" is not at all what current culture asserts it to be; in fact, in many ways, it is quite the opposite of what it's purported to be. It cannot be overstated that, as a distinction, the war on women has proven to be quite successful as a rallying cry in helping encourage and galvanize women into a powerful group and force. Over the years, radical feminists had lost momentum, and the advent of "war on women" helped reenergize this group worldwide. Using emotional vernacular and an entire nomenclature to unify and galvanize women is one thing, but using language like "war" in this regard seems woefully misguided and inaccurate. By no means should "war on women" be dismissed as pure cliché, however. For many who adopt this mantra, there is a very real war in their minds, and they perceive a battle day-to-day that needs to be waged against Bush presidency years (now Trump Presidency), Republicans, men (in general), Christianity/Religion, "masculinity, " and virtually any imagery and messaging that affirms "brutish men" or traditional values. It is not an overstatement to say hostility, and visceral hatred undergirds the collective zeal for those who describe themselves as fighting in the "war on "women," so a battle is actively waged in very real ways. Endless Women's Marches, boycotts, public shaming, doxxing, and almost all socio/cultural tactics that put others on the defensive is being used to gain an advantage over perceived adversaries. If it is asserted current targets of the collective ire of war on women advocates are misguided, who then is their actual adversary and mortal foe?

Women do indeed have a very real and formidable foe. In some instances and in many ways, it can be argued the biggest foe fighting against their advancement, legacy and progeny is (mostly unwittingly) women! This is because the primary focus of the women who adopt the prevailing parlance and narrative as their personal rallying cry, perceive the primary focus of this "war" as abortion. Abortion/infanticide has now been euphemistically characterized as "reproductive health." This demonstrates a clear and purposeful attempt to sanitize abortion, so almost any woman can get on with it as being a fundamental force toward women empowerment. Characterizing abortion in this way is flatly quite insincere, albeit it's quite effective as a talking point. Irrespective of goals, objectives, and intentions, the "war on women" with its primary focus on abortion, only helps to conveniently veil the real hostile foe and real actual war and battle. Abortion is not the root of the war on women! During battle, a fervent embrace of the truth of the battle is the way to endure sustained attacks and remain committed to defeating a foe; the cause underpinned

> ...this hateful foe is quite nefarious and diabolical because, through veiled and illogical arguments, it seduces women to accepting machinations and argumentations that actually encourage women to wage war and battle against their own interests, destiny, and progeny.

with truth paves the way for endurance and success. That said, in sustained wars, actual truth must prevail.

On the other side of every truth is a lie! This axiom is poignant because the "war on women" (with its primary focus on abortion) is, in truth, not really "the war." It is a lie. But if it's a lie, what is the truth? The truth is, there is a foe that has actually declared war on women! It is an actual force that hates women and is wholly hostile toward her. This force is committed to a conquest of ALL women and sees the woman as the cosmic battlefield that must be conquered and utterly destroyed. With sheer hatred as its motivation, this force can't destroy women outright, so it uses women to destroy women via newfangled but duplicitous arguments that actually undermine and disempower women and their capacity to wage war and win. This is the arena where this hateful foe is quite nefarious and diabolical because, through veiled and illogical arguments, it seduces women to accepting machinations and argumentations that actually encourage women to wage war and battle against their own interests, destiny, and progeny. Sadly, the actual battle destined to destroy women rages, but women are literally destroying themselves via an army of women soldiers, unwittingly fighting against women's' own interests, thus precipitating huge battlefield losses. Said differently, women are regrettably losing their respective war, but it's not due to "men," "toxic masculinity," gender bias, or any other entity that can be easily projected as "the enemy." Their battle is much more diabolical and eternal. Their battle began in "the beginning," it is eternal and cosmic, and it holds huge implications and maximum impact for all of humanity! It has been so easily concealed because it is a cosmic battle between primal issues of "good vs. "evil." The battle emanates from the unseen realm of darkness; this means, it cannot be reasoned with or mollified, it's insatiable, it's never- ending, and it's to the death! Are you ready to battle in the real war against women?

The fact is, while arguments persist about nuances and distinctions of war and the "war on women" specifically, the battle rages!

Closing Argument

Women are the target in an actual battle and war. Again, everyone is born into the war on women and based on actions, intentions, and beliefs, we are already soldiering on one side of the battle or the other. Most perceive this war as simply metaphorical and nuanced with clichéd talking points purporting the need to increase abortion on demand. But the roots of this war didn't occur and accelerate over just the past 30 years; it predates all and has morphed and accelerated from the beginning of time. Why? Why is it so focused on women? And who are the enemies and foe's? In actuality, currently perceived enemies are not the real foe. The real foe has declared war on women, and the war against them is seriously terminal... It is hatefully focused, and it is to the death! It is not nuanced; it's definitive! If women reject understanding their battle and tactual foe, they will continue to be decimated on the cosmic battlefield, and all humanity will suffer.

CHAPTER 3

THE EPIC ETERNAL BATTLE BEGINS

Opening Statement

It's a fact that women are indeed at war. Whether they perceive and understand it or not, they're in a battle for their lives. Their foe wants to dominate them and cause the maximum amount of destruction. If the outcome results in maiming their bodies, he wants it! If it's permanent damage to their soul, he wants it! If it's maximum carnage and death, he wants it! As the battle rages against them, the only way women can neutralize their ultimate foe is to unmask him in order to identify him accurately. Only then will women be able to unveil the specifics of the battle and wage war in order to turn the tide in their favor on the battlefield....

The war begins!

In order to forge a pathway of truth that confirms there is a declared "war on women," and an existential threat from a literal foe, we summarily agree with Merriam Webster's definition of war. We also tacitly agree that every war has to be declared, is characterized by battle lines and hostilities, and is undergirded by hatred and enmity. With that in mind, while they may pose threatening, boorish and other untoward behaviors toward women, base generalizations targeting "men," toxic masculinity, gender biases etc. as precipitators of war, don't actually comport with the Merriam Webster's definition; all (or even most) men are not committed mortal enemies of women. This means a collective ire toward men is misguided, and women's' actual foe continues to wreak havoc and devour unabated. That said, how is the "war on women" an actual war being waged with actual battle lines, objectives, and committed outcomes (to destroy women)? To accurately pinpoint the war and its foundations, let's take a Biblical/historical exploration of "the why," "the when," and "the where" of the actual war.

It needs to be stated again, common parlance and nomenclature around the war on women are not, by definition, legitimate. But, there is an actual ongoing eternal war that has been declared on women and is still ongoing to this very day. The oldest, best-selling, and most widely read of all historical documents is the Bible. The Bible is likely the most widely used authority in helping to confirm historical, archeological, and religious foundations accurately. That said, it is the Bible that is the final authority and source of confirmation for the war on women; it actually confirms when the war was declared, it characterizes the hatred and hostility that undergirds it the war, and why & how the battle/war on women is being waged to this very day!

The story of humanity/creation can be found in Genesis. Genesis is the first book of the Bible, and it's in Genesis that the first-ever war is declared. Notably, Genesis confirms the initiation of the war on women. Summarily, in Genesis, God speaks the world into existence, and sequentially brings forth land, vegetation, and living creatures. On the sixth day, God declares His desire to create man in His own image and creates Adam (man), then Eve (woman). Since they were created in God's image, Adam and Eve were essentially deemed the "god's" of this world, crowned with full power, creativity, and authority, exacting God's image and likeness in the earth! It was their subsequent dereliction and rebellion that subverted their power and authority and, in doing so, enshrined and enthroned a mortal enemy committed to waging...War! Parenthetically, the significance and purpose of the book of Genesis cannot be overstated. Every single line and verse presents significant and exhaustive illumination into the mind, heart, and purposes of God. Summarily providing the Genesis creation account (depicted here) doesn't provide thorough theological or exegetic context and Biblical accuracy. But, further exposition would take us too far afield from the main point of this book. I implore you to please read the entire book of Genesis for a more thorough illumination of creation.

The Biblical account of creation is vitally important because it definitively confirms the fundamental pivot point of the actual war that now confronts humanity. To be sure, Genesis confirms all things God created were in perfect harmony, the world was in bliss and without lack, the rulers of this world (Adam & Eve) were equals in power and authority, and all was perfect. Then came a serpent. The serpent in Genesis is representative of satan (lucifer; fallen angel cast out of the heavens). It is the serpent that seduced and undermined the rulers of this world to rebel against and disobey God's command (to not eat from a forbidden tree), and when they succumbed and rebelled, their power and authority were appropriately ceded to the serpent. (As with any kingdom, when a ruler or king rebels against its owns edicts in order to accommodate whims of another kingdom, it cedes power and authority to the other. The ruler then becomes subservient to that other kingdom. Put plainly, when Adam and Eve rebelled against their King (God) in deference to another kingdom (serpent/demonic realm), they ceded their divine power and authority to the other realm. It was as if they symbolically took off their respective royal crowns, bowed, and cast them before the king of another kingdom; this act enshrined and enthroned the other kingdom, and since that time, the world's equilibrium was cast into perpetual chaos.

Theologians and scholars have debated for centuries whether the serpent in the Bible was an actual serpent or some allegorical representation of the demonic realm. Whether actual or allegorical can be argued and debated, but what is not debated is that God declared this was war. The first war declared in the Bible was between the woman and the serpent, it would be an eternal (ongoing) battle and the war between kingdoms (God's Kingdom vs. satan's) started in eternity-past now manifests in this realm. The war now culminates with human beings (used as vessels on either side) to exact the cosmic war for humanity vs. the serpent of the demonic realm.

The single act of rebellion in the garden is quite significant because it is the fundamental pivot of why we now live in a "fallen world," why satan is deemed "the god of this world" (2 Cor 4:4), the "ruler of this world" (John 12:31) and the "prince of the power of the air" (Eph 2:2). When cast down into this realm, satan certainly did not start out this way. He schemed, used cunning and guile, to undermine God's creation in order to gain a modicum of delegated authority and control in this realm.

To be sure, the Garden of Eden and world were indeed perfect at inception, but the world has digressed to the degree its commonplace that "bad things happen," sickness, disease, drought, famines, pestilence, and all other known world atrocities now occur regularly; the cost of human suffering is beyond what we can compute, and it's all due to a change in authority (Adam & Eve dereliction) and sin. The new ruler and "god of this world" has been enthroned via rebellion. The opening for rebellion and sin in this realm was also the beginning of the declared war against God's creation, and most notably, it's when the war on women begins!

As stated, the definition of war requires elements of a declared war, an enemy, hostilities, enmity, hatred and etc. That said, after Adam and Eve sinned, they not only conferred their "rulership" to another kingdom (satanic realm), God dutifully conveyed consequences (for the serpent and Adam & Eve) going forward. Genesis 3:14-15 (MSG) confirms,

> God told the serpent:
> "Because you've done this (tempted Eve to eat of the tree), you're cursed, cursed beyond all cattle and wild animals, Cursed to slink on your belly and eat dirt all your life I'm declaring war between you and the Woman, between your offspring and hers, He'll wound your head, you'll wound his heel."

Please note, while the Bible is full of wars, rumors of wars, and countless battles and conquests, this is the first war declared in the Bible! This is significant because, in actuality, ALL wars and battles (from then until now) fundamentally stem from this one. Equilibrium and homeostasis for all creation were disrupted with the change in power and authority, and that was bad enough. But God went further and declared to the serpent, *"I'm declaring war between you and the Woman, between your offspring and hers. He'll wound your head, you'll wound his heel."* What is the significance of this? Why would God declare an eternal war between woman and serpent over a simple misstep of rebellion? Firstly, since God is omniscient (knows ALL things), omnipotent (is ALL powerful), and omnipresent (eternal; preexistent outside of time and space), His declaration was in a prophetic voice. God's proclamation was merely confirmation that since Adam & Eve ceded their power and authority, going forward, they would suffer severe consequences from their foe (this was a matter of fact, especially since satan hates God and all His creation).

15

He appropriately deemed it as war because it fully characterizes the zeal of satan's fight, and resulting consequences and Adam & Eve's plight.

God declared the fact that due to a change in power and authority in this realm, there would be a war on women. But, the war against God and all His creation was already raging. Lucifer was cast out of the heavens, relegated to this realm, impotent and utterly powerless. The only way to power was through cunning and seduction that would undermine the rulership and authority of Adam and Eve. Make no mistake, the demonic realm holds a deep hatred for God's Kingdom and all His creation, and therefore were already waging cosmic and eternal war! I surmise God affirmed the declaration of the war on women for the following strategic reasons: 1. God wanted to confirm severe consequences for sin/rebellion 2. God wanted women forevermore to be fully sensitized and wary of "cunning" and "seduction"; extra sensitivity is supposed to help shield, protect and help stave off demonic assaults against themselves and offspring 3. God knew the world would arrive at a point in time when women and children would be utterly and mercilessly targeted for destruction, and He foreknew it would be critically important for us to definitively confirm who is waging war against women, when it started, and how the demonic realm has targeted them for obliteration and total destruction. Our ability to confirm these Biblical facts is supposed to encourage and embolden us to do all we can to help battle and win the "war on women" (and her offspring)! That said, Adam and Eve's dereliction was no "simple misstep," this culminated in a transition of power between kingdoms at war (Kingdom of heaven vs. kingdom of hell) that had been started in "eternity past" in the heavenly realms. Lucifer and his minions lost their attempt to rebel and overthrow God and were cast out and relegated to this (earthly) realm. With limited pathways to achieving his lust for power and rulership over his own kingdom, satan plotted to deceive Gods' image-bearers as a pathway to his own throne His scheme involved getting Adam and Eve to defer and acquiesce to his authority; he'd suborn those whom God made in His image, and receive their power and authority. After obtaining conferred authority to rule and reign in this realm (authority granted to Adam and Eve), he would engage in more eternal acts of rebellion by waging war in this realm against God. Satan used cunning and seduction to precipitate Adam and Eve's acquiescence; it is understood, when a "king" appeases, and acquiescence's in obedience and deference to another kingdom, he subjugates his power and empowers the other. In the end, stiff consequences Adam and Eve are due to God's chagrin at the transition of His power away from those He walked with daily (and who were bearing His image). It should be noted, the most terminal consequences for all of humanity is the literal beginning of satan's "war on women." From the very beginning of mankind, satan was, is, and will always be, the consummate hater and mortal foe of all women! Now he has the power to do something about it!

It is now clear that satan is our mortal foe. The Bible clearly reveals and factually uncovers unmitigated truth about the actual war on women. It confirms the war was declared, is typified with only two conflicting sides, (satan/demonic realm vs. woman and her offspring), and it is being waged in order to decimate and destroy women and children to this very day! To prevent salient background information and historical grounding of facts from being lost, here again, is a summary of what the Bible confirms: Through the ancient text of the most prominent historical reference, the Bible, we discovered that as a result of rebellion and disobedience, a new and quite destructive kingdom was ushered in. The new kingdom undermined God's rulers (Adam and Eve), who were ordained with free-will and power and authority in the earthly realm. Kingdomology portends that when Adam & Eve were cunningly seduced and went against God's warning and admonishment to not "eat from the tree of knowledge of good and evil" (Gen 2:17), " delegated power and authority" that was given to them, was then transitioned to another kingdom (satan's kingdom/ the demonic realm). Now the serpent/satan has become "god/ruler of this world." Adam and Eve's disobedience to creator God immediately confirmed them as obedient servants of another god; again, there are only two sides, and because they are diametrically opposed, either side mutually excludes the other. Adam and Eve's reprobation also permanently ensconced and cemented disobedience as a fundamental human instinct. Since this was not God's design, He meted out and confirmed obvious consequences. One of the consequences is that women and offspring will be in a perpetual battle for their lives in a war against satan. This battle begins with the targeting of women and offspring, but also extends as the primary assault satan makes against God and all of humanity. In satan's feeble but quite cunning mind, because women represent the "door" to all

17

of humanity (i.e. virtually every human that has existed, has been born of a woman), he thinks he can achieve victory over God and His creation via the unrelenting attacks on "the woman and her offspring." For him, the consummate cosmic battleground and war are wholly fought via the woman and respective offspring. This is clearly not trivial and has now evolved into a war of cosmic proportions. To be sure, this cosmic war is what culminates in much of the human suffering and destruction we see around the world today, as women and children are maligned and targeted in the worst (most heinous) ways for utter destruction.

The fact is, through ignorance of the battle, many are literally warring against themselves on behalf of their mortal enemy; this may sound too definitive because most are ignorant of the intricacies of this war, and therefore cannot know the extent to which they are being used. But, because there are only two sides to this war, it IS truly definitive!

Like all other wars, the war on women is indeed binary (only two competing parts). People will either fight and battle for the women and their offspring or are actually battling for (and dutifully enthrone) satan. The fact is, through ignorance of the battle, many are literally warring against themselves on behalf of their mortal enemy; this may sound too definitive because most are ignorant of the intricacies of this war, and therefore cannot know the extent to which they are being used. But, because there are only two sides to this war, it IS truly definitive! Binary choices mean we are on one side or another; there is no middle ground, nor alternative reality whereby one can perch as just an "innocent" non-committed observer. Everyone, all of humanity, is automatically enlisted into this cosmic battle and wittingly or unwittingly fighting for one side or the other. The Bible confirms the battle was raging before we were born, and it will continue rage when we're gone. The satanic realm is unrelenting, tireless, and has great momentum. Due to the subtle deceptions and nuances, the enemy has been masterful in using humanity as the primary weapon against itself! His side continues to gain momentum, and indications are, he is winning as he is further enthroned and entrenched via relative ignorance to the battle.

After the battlefield foe and enemy is revealed, some of the other issues that need to be understood in order to effectively fight (and win) any war are, what are the weapons/tools that our enemy is using against us? Is the enemy heavily armed, and based on his weaponry, are we vulnerable to his attacks? What weapons do we have to be used to "counter-attack?" What are our primary weapons of the battle, and how can we help win in the fight? The answers to these questions are better understood with a purposeful review of God's view of the significance of women. While some have complained and try to assert God sees women as unequal and subservient, Biblical facts confirm God made women to be quite a significant key factor to his Kingdom order. He relies heavily upon women, as they have been designed as the perfect vessel and conduit for birthing and nurturing humanity. In God's mind, women are not subservient afterthoughts; they are critical in His plans for all of humanity! Certainly, since God hold women in such high regard with such a central role for all of humanity, our foe will dutifully regard women as the primary enemy target and the ultimate "prize of war," especially if he can get her to rebel and undermine God. With grotesque evil emanating from his feeble mind, our mortal foe believes that by pursuing and targeting women for utter destruction, he can prevent God's ultimate plans for humanity. While delusions of grandeur about ruling and reigning in his own kingdom stricken him, the woman (God's chosen vessel for all humanity) smitten's him!

Now that it has been unveiled that the root of the cosmic war revolves around satan's battle plans, and women are his primary target, humanity must be wise enough to perceive the battle and fully prepare to engage in the war so that we may change the trajectory of the battle. With active engagement to thwart satan, we find womankind is not only God's chosen door to humanity, but they also hold the strategic keys to winning in the cosmic battle....

Closing Argument

The bible declares, "Then you will know the truth and the truth will set you free" ~

Jn 8:32. The truth is, satan is the existential foe! He has targeted women for total destruction. None are innocent observers of the war declared against women. We are already fighting on one side of the war on women, or the other. Unwittingly, many have taken up arms with our principal foe to fight against our best interests (humanity). Now we have the capacity to choose to adjust perspective in order to orient thoughts and actions around the truth that satan IS the foe who is systemically destroying women and offspring. Our foe hates God and all His creation, and since battle lines have been drawn, he focuses on targeting God and all humanity through "the woman and her offspring." The question we need to ask ourselves at this point is, which side of the battle are we (individually) on? Are we on satan's side of the battle as he uses cunning and schemes to destroy women utterly? Or, are we on God's side of the battle fighting for women and respective offspring?

CHAPTER 4

GATEWAY TO HUMANITY: WOMAN-KIND

Opening Statement

Aristotle once said, "Justice in this sense, then, is not part of virtue but virtue entire, nor is the contrary injustice part of vice but vice entire."[1] We hear and read much said about virtuous women; God designed them to be that way. Today, however, we observe an onslaught of women embracing all kinds of vice, wholly incongruent with justice and virtue. It's time to examine how we have arrived at a point in history when women gleefully cheer vice, at the expense and rejection of virtue that impacts their destiny.

Since the Bible is the most accurate historical document beginning with creation, we now know that God confirmed a declaration of war, and it is our foe who has been fervently waging war against women to destroy them utterly. It is now known that the very first declared war had women as the primary target for annihilation. The question is, why? What is the significance of women? Why women?

If we think deeply about why our foe targets women for utter annihilation, the answer becomes obvious. All human life comes through

---

[1] *Aristotle, Nicomachean Ethics, Book V, Chapter 1*

a woman! This is not at all a slight to men, but factually speaking, God designed human beings and our process of becoming to include being formed, nurtured, and then born through the womb of women. To understand the root of the war on women, it is fundamental that the intricacies and processes connected to women (and inherent vitality to all humanity) are not to be overlooked or ignored.

God designed women to be curators and incubators of life. Since the beginning of all humankind, the curating and incubating process has proven to be scientifically precise, irreducibly flawless, and an empirically beautiful celebration of life as it unfolds. All of this precision and beauty culminates inside the woman. With such a powerful testament to humankind, there's no doubt women carry the "weight" of glory (literally and figuratively) that continues to unfold as it is born and adopted into creation! Considering this, it should be no surprise that satan would focus and target his vile hatred and schemes of destruction on women. Women are the principals for birthing and multiplying God's creation, and satan hates God and His creation (especially humankind, since it's the only part of Gods creation created in the "image and likeness" of God; as "image- bearers," we constantly remind satan of God and the fullness of His glory and grace!). Therefore, all humankind is the primary target of satan's schemes for destruction. Via women, our foe rages against all humankind; this is especially true as we fulfill God's mandate to "be fruitful and multiply."

As we multiply, we (at least theoretically) expand the cosmic battlefield. With more humankind being born, there are more of God's "image bearers" to contend with as they are being illuminated on the cosmic battlefield. Therefore, demonism rampages with "the woman and her offspring" in its sight.

> *Since the beginning of all humankind, the curating and incubating process has proven to be scientifically precise, irreducibly flawless, and an empirically beautiful celebration of life as it unfolds..*

If we are to begin pushing back and waging war against our foe, having a keen awareness of our foe's battlefield strategy prevents susceptibility to his guile and subtleties. A strategic weapon satan has been masterful at cultivating and leveraging, is "culture." Culture, more importantly, a wholly manipulated and beguiled culture, is a powerful weapon and tool for the demonic realms' battle against women. Through culture, our foe can infuse schemes and tools of manipulation that just possess "half-truths," and drive the start of social revolution (cultural monikers like "Social justice" and "women's right to choose" movements are perhaps good examples of this). It is vital to becoming observant of how satan leverages culture and society to malign and bring devastation upon women. The Bible confirms and distinguishes satan as "liar," "deceiver," "cunning," "scheming," "evil," "vile," and an almost endless list of other negative characterizations. True to his name, he tactically uses his guile and cunning in order to deceive the masses.

As mentioned, our foe seeks control of hearts and minds through purposeful perversions and mischaracterization of truth and facts. Think about it, if he can beguile and manipulate women to not procreate because of purported "global warming," he wins. In this case, he wins because God seeks that humankind is being fruitful and multiplying more "image-bearers", while our foe seeks to use " environmentalism" (something mankind definitively cannot control) to control tendencies toward procreation so as to minimize humanity in order to reduce and/or eliminate warriors on the cosmic battlefield. Likewise, if he can get women to reject and project their collective ire on men/misogyny/toxic masculinity, he wins. With this tactic, our foe projects men as purveyors of all women's woes, and as such, infuses the idea they should be totally rejected; this again plays into our foe's strategy to reduce procreation while encouraging lesbianism, which also reduces healthy family units. Additionally, if he can get women to believe a baby being formed in the womb is just a "clump of cells" to be discarded at any time based on mere "convenience," he wins. This is satan's ultimate affront to God; as he manipulates God's children to self-eliminate/reject God's own handiwork of new additions to His creation (i.e. babies); satan "spits" in the face of God and (no doubt) boasts that God's own children are rejecting His most precious handiworks! Further, if satan can mislead "the Church" (Parishioners & Clergy) into believing they shouldn't participate civically (i.e. vote), and if they do, they would be compelled to empower/vote for people who are more than willing to overlook issues of God's creation (via abortion/infanticide), he wins! The most telling example of dubious manipulation is satan's use of God's "body" (the Church) as a weapon aligned against itself on his (satan's) side of the battlefield; he uses the Church by taking advantage of voting traditions and sensitivities. In the end, our foe has blinded the church (in general) to subvert Biblical voting, and instead vote based on ideology and "Party" (notably, the Political Party aligned on his side of the battlefield). While satan deserves nothing but God's wrath and complete rejection, admittedly, he has been masterful in manipulating the cosmic battlefield in his favor. Make no mistake, in almost every area of life, our foe uses cunning to deceive and delude. And in almost every arena, we (as actual targets of his hatred) actually facilitate him as he decimates and conquers the cosmic battlefield.

Food for thought: God can have our heart while satan has our attention

With innate God-given instincts for self-preservation, our principal foe knows women (and humankind in general) will never opt to wage war against themselves and willingly destroy themselves purposely; but, he is cunning enough to realize that through tactics of seduction, lies and grotesque deceptions, he can accomplish almost anything against humankind! This includes actually turning his war against women against itself by using women to battle on his side of the battle lines. Through his tactics, we now observe the fervent extent to which women willingly (but unwittingly) declare war on themselves wearing satan's "war on women" manipulation as a badge of honor. Unfortunately, this only serves to cast women into a perpetual chaotic cycle of self-destruction.

How are so many wholly deceived as to precipitate in their own demise? Let's be clear, lies and deception are satan's weapons for waging war. Think about it, if he deceived Adam and Eve out of their prescribed authority and rulership (even as they walked hand-in-hand and face-to-face with God daily), surely he knows he can use the same cunning ways of seduction to concoct schemes that further enshrine and enthrone his kingdom as he wages a diabolical war to destroy "the woman and her offspring utterly". When demonic deceptions morph, spread, and picks up momentum, the enemy begins to win in his war on women. With the embrace of today's socially accepted nomenclature of the "war on women," we've arrived at a time in world history when women are now literally destroying themselves (and their progeny). How, exactly, does the mortal enemy and hater of all women accomplish using women to actually destroy themselves? We willingly destroy ourselves by embracing a concerted, persistent history of subtle deceptions. Our foe has attained what should have been impossible for intelligent beings who are inclined toward God. But, humanity has now digressed to the extent many are smitten and in full embrace of ideological zeal that undermines our ability to stand on God's side and appropriately battle in satan's war on women. Montesquieu wrote in *The Spirit of the Laws,* 1748: "In a popular state, one spring more is necessary, namely, virtue ... The politic Greeks, who lived under a popular government, knew no other support than virtue ...When virtue is banished, ambition invades the minds of those who are disposed to receive it, and avarice possesses the whole community." What we are seeing and experiencing in our foe's war on women today is a complete lack of virtue and an overwhelming sense of avarice! We need a collective wake up call to the true extent of what's at stake with the "war on women."

The socially accepted parlance surrounding the war on women is the ultimate misnomer. Again, the moniker "war on women" is a relatively new distinction that was designed to help coalesce women into a unified and fully galvanized base that could begin to speak and act as a powerful, even "cultural," force. With traditional cultural feminism seemingly hitting a plateau and losing potency and popularity within certain segments of women, there was a need for new central themes that were passionate, emotional, and seemingly empowering to all women in all demographics. This messaging had to be inviting to sub-groups that were not outspoken proponents of "modern feminism" (like, for instance, suburban and "religious" women). Coalescing unified coalitions of women operating under specific agreed-upon banner and cause (in this case, "war on women") allowed the culmination of a reinvigorated new movement; thus, "war on women" nomenclature evolved as the newest feminist distinction connoting the need for women get involved a virtual war to combat and battle what they perceive as hostile, even hateful forces.

As it turns out, the fundamental idea behind the war on women's movement is used to harness collective power to push for changes into myriad social/cultural issues designed to empower women as they execute (and win) the "war." But in actuality, our foe used this movement to gain momentum as a strategy and means of devouring all women. He harnesses their heightened agitation and turns their collective angst to be used against themselves on his side of the battlefield. With women actually embracing a declaration of war against themselves (and their best interests), satan bolsters and accelerates his scheme to destroy women and, by extension, humanity utterly.

Fundamentally, the root of the war on women culminated in the beginning (in the garden of Eden). As satan sharpened his focus on ways to express his jealous rage and hate for God and humanity, he concocted a ruse by seducing and beguiling Adam and Eve that resulted in them ceding their kingdom power and authority to him. Upon becoming "prince of the power of the air" and "ruler of this world," satan launched headlong into undermining God through His most precious creation, humankind. Since women are strategic to the multiplication of God's creation, satan has waged a targeted and very focused battle against women and offspring in order to thwart and undermine God. If creation can be stymied and reduced, satan gains strategic advantage on the cosmic battlefield and poses an ultimate affront to God (using His creation, to fight on the side of evil). In all, satan's goal is to undermine God and all humanity under the guise of "the war on woman"; under this ruse, he aggressively executes his war plans destined to decimate "the woman and her offspring."

As our foe's manipulations of current culture have tilted the battlefield significantly in his favor, we can discern the root of his war a subsequent "fruit" of his efforts are now manifest. With the fate of women and offspring targeted and on the precipice of annihilation, will we generally remain complicit as he presses his insatiable quest to conquer, possess and devour the fruit of his diabolical war? Think about it, with what has been revealed about the foe in the war on women and resulting "feminist" movements embraced by churches/religions, well-intended "people of Faith" can already have pledged their heart as a servant God, but (due to their ignorance of satan's war) at the same time, actively engage in waging war as a soldier on satan's side battlefield! This is an incredible paradox. God can have the heart of man, but our foe who actively tries to destroy man can have our undivided attention as we "soldier on" on his side of the battle against God and humanity!

> *...satan's goal is to undermine God and all humanity under the guise of "the war on woman"; under this ruse, he aggressively executes his war plans destined*

How do we begin to unpack the significance of what has been unveiled about this war and the revelations therein? The revelation of the roots of our mortal foe's' war against us requires a response. Where do we start? Other than now having the capacity to observe, there is nothing we can do about the root of this war; it is eternally cemented and predates all of humanity. But, we can do something about satan's "fruit of war." We can neutralize his spoils. We can start by euphemistically "cleaning the fruit"; this represents a pivotal first step toward winning the battle.

Closing Argument

Most have at least unwittingly participated in satan's war against women. He's used tactics of language and deceptions to embolden an army fiercely fighting on his side of the battlefield against God and all of humanity. Our foe has always been a master deceiver. Ultimately though, as satan's battlefield tactics and strategy come more into focus, mankind is forced to make a binary choice. On one side, satan's evils continue to be embraced, and his attacks on womankind escalate unabated. On the other side, mankind can embrace God's side of the battle by rejecting satan's "war on women" nomenclature and associated cultural schemes. Again, only two sides!
There is no middle ground! We either commit to standing on God's side, or we're (by default) fighting for the other.....

PART II
"FRUIT" OF THE WAR

Counting the Spoils

CHAPTER 5

MODERN FEMINISM: BATTLE FOR HARVEST OF RIPENED FRUIT

Opening Statement

"It seems sometimes as if the foundations of the nation were becoming rotten, and Christians seem to act as if they thought God did not see what they do in politics (civic engagement). But I tell you, he does see it, and he will bless or curse this nation, according to the course they take."
~Charles Finney[2]

Our foe (satan) is committed to our mutual destruction. He hates us, he hates God, and he hates every earthly thing! He is waging war against humankind by using humankind (in our collective ignorance and dereliction) to declare war against itself. The currently accepted "war on women" parlance is, in actuality, the war against ourselves. It will take strident resolve to fight against the raging tide of accepted nomenclature, duplicitous cultural forces, and radical social movements. If we are to deny our demented foe of his fruit of war, these are the arenas we must fight!

---

[2]   *Charles Finney wrote in Lecture XV "Hindrances to Revival" Revival Lectures, 185)*

The "harvest" of big battleground wins and ultimate payoff in satan's war on women come as he overwhelms and devours the "fruit" produced by the diabolical root of his war. For him, the fruit is any destructive actions, behaviors, or attitudes he can cement into the hearts and minds of humanity that helps undermine women and offspring. Knowing our foe is hateful, the father of lies and a wretched accuser, he uses any demonstration that humanity actually fights on his side of the battle and against their creator, as justification to God that all of humanity deserves "judgment" and must be destroyed. (Thank God for His mercies and loving- kindness toward us) Make no mistake, at this point in history, satan is further emboldened as he amps up attacks and assaults as the ultimate affront to God. When he can assert much of God's creation (mankind) willfully fights for him and against God almighty on his demonic side of the battle, he mocks, laughs, and boasts.

If there were a way to deceive women into believing and embracing that it is virtuous, noble and truly progressive to reject traditional norms of motherhood and matriarchy, surely this would be the deception the sworn enemy of women would use to win in his war against them. Using deceptive mindsets that preclude God's mandate of being fruitful and multiplying, while also rejecting roles that help build healthy homes and family legacy, is the perfect plot for the mortal enemy of women. Sadly, but truthfully, modern-day "feminism" has transformed into a movement that wholly comports with the diabolical schemes of our mortal enemy.

... the fruit is any destructive actions, behaviors, or attitudes he can cement into the hearts and minds of humanity that helps undermine women and offspring

It should be noted, this book is not written to address the full deconstruction and anthropology of feminism and associated history. There are already many books that have helped deconstruct the history of triumphs and fails of many great women and associated relevance to the feminist movement. My scant knowledge on the subject of "feminism," as a movement, couldn't reproduce necessary scholarship and thoughtful analysis; at best, my thoughts in the matter would be redundant and incomplete compared to the many thoughtful scholars who have already dutifully provided thorough history and analysis on feminism. There is one goal of this book, and that is to convey the actual war on women from "the root to the fruit." This obviously has to segue into feminism but is not fundamentally about the feminist movement. It's about women as a "target" and battleground for a real war being waged against them. That said, this book has given special emphasis to move the conversation and needed context about the real "war on women," forward. Even with feminisms colorful and (in some cases) inglorious history, satan's "war on women" is the most vital issue!

The "war on women" from the context of its actual beginning, its roots through to its modern-day fruit of neo-feminism/"radical feminism," is not actually evolutionary! In many ways, viewing women's movements as evolutions that pace to an ever-evolving next level trajectory is perhaps one of the most significant false reveals about women's movements. The reality is, viewing women's movements in this way conceals the fact that this war has been declared and waged from the beginning of humankind. Viewing women's challenges as strictly evolutionary is another deception that the enemy cleverly uses to project the fault on others while precipitating a mindset of consistent victimhood that then perpetuates a need for continual redress. Concealed in the progression of feminism is the demonic realm that actually drives the entire ontological deception by aggressively pushing for more agitation and ever- increasing progress; aggressive perpetual motion provides the sense of forward motion, but doesn't provide the ability to adequately reflect and take inventory of progress and success that have actually been made. Our foe constantly focuses efforts on fomenting raw emotions like hatred and resentment, so women remain gripped and swept into a perpetual state of being emotionally triggered while pushing his battlefield agenda. Make no mistake, our enemy's need to project delusions are essential in his effort to veil and conceal his real war destined to destroy all women; he has been masterfully waging this war for millennia's, and other than a great acceleration of success via "war on women" subculture, nothing much has changed. Women and offspring are still being maligned and destroyed at increasing rates. Even with momentum on our foe's his side of the battlefield however, God's grace and mercies have kept and protected women as, even with the onslaught of the foe, they have incredibly progressed indeed.

Since women are God's strategic vessels used as the fulcrum to birth God's image and likeness in expanding humanity, it's clear God has protected and graced women to have a rich history and legacy. Throughout history, God has raised great women and deposited in them burning zeal and concern about the rights and status of women; some of these historical figures began great and impactful women's movements in the 1800s. To gain a proper perspective, it is important to reflect on progress women achieved in the past.

Necessary changes began to occur for women when divine destiny hoisted powerfully principled women out of obscurity and onto the world stage to confront the hostility, aggressions, and gross inequality toward women. This precipitated the beginning of the women's suffrage movement. Feminist Mary Wollstonecraft, born in Spitalfields, London, in 1759, began advocating equality for women long before the height of the women's suffrage movement in the United States. "Though she is perhaps best known as the mother of Mary Shelley, who wrote the classic novel 'Frankenstein: The Modern Prometheus,' Wollstonecraft was a prominent author in her own right. Her most famous work, 'A Vindication of the Rights of Woman,' was published in 1792 and circulated several decades later by American suffragists Elizabeth Cady Stanton and Susan B. Anthony in their newspaper, Revolution. Wollstonecraft advocated education reform as a means of empowering women and argued that the education system had been designed to oppress women, undermining their formation in a way that prevented them not only from flourishing as wives and mothers, but also blocking them from entering professional fields.

Conservative Feminism is not an oxymoron. Wollstonecraft believed that empowered women would embrace motherhood and described women who fulfilled their responsibilities as 'independent.' According to Wollstonecraft, women's first duty "is to themselves as rational creatures" and secondly 'as citizens, is that, which includes so many, of a mother.' Wollstonecraft viewed abortion as a depraved consequence of society's failure to recognize the intrinsic value of women, as well as of the prevailing attitude that women should be objectified and subjugated by men. She described women and children as victims of this failure to value women and motherhood: Women becoming, consequently, weaker, in mind and body ... have not sufficient strength to discharge the first duty of a mother; and sacrificing to lasciviousness the parental affection, that ennobles instinct, either destroy the embryo in the womb, or cast it off when born. Wollstonecraft promoted pro-life ideas in her writing, but she also embodied the sacrifices she wrote about in her own life as a single mother, having her first child, Fanny Imlay, out of wedlock despite the harsh judgment of society."[3] Early feminists were strident about protecting the rights of unborn human life, and it impacted the personal stance historically notable men.

With the momentum of the anti-slavery movements led by President Abraham Lincoln and the honorable Frederick Douglass, women's suffrage movements were launched and spread. Notably, as the pioneer of Civil Rights, Frederick Douglass was a proponent and advocate for women's suffrage; he pioneered fighting for human dignity and civil rights for all, and the women's suffrage movement was also part of his fight.

With clear hostilities, hatred, and notable enemies (including laws and precedent) targeted at women, Women's suffrage was seen and internalized as an actual battle and war. One example that demonstrates how women internalized their fight and plight in the battle for women is, in the popular 1964 movie Mary Poppins, Mrs. Banks sang: "We're clearly soldiers in petticoats And dauntless crusaders for woman's votes Though we adore men individually We agree that as a group they're rather stupid! Cast off the shackles of yesterday! Shoulder to shoulder into the fray! Our daughters' daughters will adore us and they'll sing in grateful chorus 'Well done, Sister Suffragette!'" The suffrage movement gained great support worldwide, creating a push to amend the U.S. Constitution.

A prominent leader in the women's suffrage movement was Susan B. Anthony. Susan B. Anthony had a fervent desire to see women simply become equal in stature and influence as men! She worked tirelessly to help illuminate the rigors and woes of all women, and in doing so, she also became a beacon of light and hope for Black women who were raped, abused, and treated as mere "property" as a result of being enslaved. There were many being maligned and abused due to slavery, and this led to the abolitionist/civil rights movement and the women's suffrage movements to align closely. Frederick Douglass and Susan B. Anthony became friends

---

[3] *Daily Signal, Jeanne Mancini, "Early Feminists Were right About Unborn Human Life" January 03 2020*

and contemporaries, as it became ever more clear that abolitionist goals and women's suffrage goals aligned as basic human rights goals!

With her immense works and successes in changing the trajectory for women, Susan B. Anthony has been dutifully heralded as a pioneer and American heroine for all. Her contributions are timeless; because of her effort(s), new Amendments to the U.S. Constitution (and laws and ordinances thereof) were passed. President Gerald Ford praised her, February 13, 1976: "Susan B. Anthony ... with other dedicated women ... took the cause of women's suffrage to State capitals across our growing Nation ... The irreversible change she wrought ... led to the ratification of the Nineteenth Amendment." It should be known that her zeal for women was not her only contribution to American society. Due to intemperance, lack of moderation, and rampant abuses women endured at the hands of drunk men, Susan B. Anthony also fought to prohibit alcohol, stating in her address to the Daughters of Temperance, March 1, 1849: "Ladies! There is no Neutral position for us ... If we sustain not this noble enterprise ... then is our influence on the side of Intemperance. If we say we love the Cause and then sit down at our ease, surely does our action speak the lie. And now permit me once more to beg of you to lend your aid to this great Cause, the Cause of God and all Mankind." With her immense success and all her accomplishments for women, the most notable attribute of Ms. Anthony is that she was a mighty woman of God, and due to her tireless dedication, He used her mightily!

Women's suffrage leader Julia Ward Howe was the first woman member of the American Academy of Arts and Letters. She also felt a palpable battle and war was being wrought as she fought for women. She wrote The Battle Hymn of the Republic, stating in the 3rd verse: "I have read a fiery gospel writ in burnished rows of steel; 'As ye deal with my contemnors, so with you my grace shall deal; LET THE HERO, BORN OF WOMAN, crush the serpent with his heel, Since God is marching on." After reflecting on the instantiation of satan's war against women, this verse is quite prescient!

Even with great power and nobility of women who began women suffrage in order to bring attention to the disparity and plight of women, we now know the war on women actually began well before them. No, it didn't evolve from the pioneering efforts of powerful women like Elizabeth Cady Stanton, Susan B. Anthony and others during the woman's suffrage movement in the 1880s. This movement was indeed important and necessary, as women were indeed being treated horribly and abused without restraint; these efforts necessarily raised issues surrounding equal rights, human sensibilities and new laws that would then protect women, and they were a conduit to positive changes God ordained so that the onslaught of satanic attacks on women would be lessened. It would be easy to summarize that women's rights in America simply evolved from women's suffrage, then to women's liberation, then to modern feminism, to now a more radical brand of feminism that culminates in the "war on women" orthodoxy and nomenclature. But the war didn't begin with women's suffrage and the needs and protections of women didn't just ramp up in response to more and more power and protections for women. History confirms Women were being mistreated well before the 1800s. It also confirms women the paradigm of being targeted, mistreated, abused, and even killed will never end. While progress was being made in the 1900s and 2000s, for many women that progress was much too slow and incremental. This is when satan's deceptions went into overdrive; he targeted the other notable object of his unfettered hatred, the baby.

Remember, Genesis 3 confirms "…war between the woman and her offspring…". Alas, the baby once again comes into focus, and in these ensuing centuries (1900-2000's), satan "amped up" and agitated women to ever-increasing levels of insatiable zeal, turning to hostility, then to radicalism …. against the baby! With the many distractions of life and rampant cultural/secular relativism, satan's fundamental deceptive ploy that is now producing much "fruit," comes from his being able to keep women focused on "forward-projecting" agitation, and on conquering incessant "shadows" that can never be apprehended or assuaged. With this, they lose perspective of being god's chosen vessels to nurture humanity, and instead become wholly emotional, despondent, grief-stricken, and resigned to the extent they become incapable of historical prudence and logical introspection. Our foe's ability to masterfully overwhelm women in a way that makes them unable to focus on what really matters, so they move away from personal values and common sense, precipitates "the offspring" (baby) to be viewed as mere collateral (merely an inconvenient "means to an end"). And, it is the offspring that is ultimately "sacrificed!"

Now that our foe's assault against God and humanity can be confirmed and is indeed manifest, dutiful introspection is in order. As Dr. Ravi Zacharias asserts, "Worldview must answer individual questions in correspondence to reality, and the sum of all answers must be coherent." That said, the question at the moment is, "Can you reconcile what has been unveiled about our foe, the war and battlefield into a consistently coherent worldview you can stridently live by?

Closing Argument

Over the generations, women have made great strides toward once again being viewed as "equals" with men. They have not been able to take inventory of their successes, however, as our foe uses an incessant, insatiable agitation to drive a new cultural embrace of his deceptive scheme using the nomenclature of the "war on women." He has created a cunning scheme to devour women (and children), while in actuality, he uses women's zeal for justice as a rallying cry for them to gleefully cheer and fight to be at war with themselves. In the end, they gleefully and wantonly succumb to secular humanist calls to sacrifice themselves and their progeny....

CHAPTER 6

HARVESTING "FRUIT OF WAR": OUR FOE'S NECESSARY SACRIFICE....

Opening Statement

I'm declaring war between you and the Woman,
between your offspring and hers.
He'll wound your head, you'll wound his heel."
~ Genesis 3:15 (MSG).

At the beginning, the war was declared and has been effectively waged against women and offspring. Through the use of unconscionable injustices, maltreatment and child sacrifices, satan has overwhelmed and decimated women and children as he assaults God and all of creation. The battle is now "white-hot" and "the woman and her offspring" are on the precipice....

Many women may proclaim they'll fight "the hordes of hell" to burnish and bask at any enemies who would attempt to malign and destroy them. But what if it is literal hordes of hell that have deceived these same women to actually enshrine and encourage modalities of modern feminism purposely concocted to disempower them? If they knew better, would women willingly fight with, and alongside, satanic evils explicitly designed to destroy and undermine women? If the current orthodoxy of modern feminism is built on satanic lies and deceit in order to destroy women, would women (even after coming to know the truth) still fight to precipitate their own demise? These are not rhetorical questions. These are the heart of the matter. We are now confirming inconvenient truths about the war on women. Asking oneself these questions at this point is important because they are the crux of the matter. The facts confirmed to this point, there is a literal war being waged with, against, and most importantly, inside of women. Since women can perceive and realize their hateful foe's tactics and strategies of his war, the war can now take on new urgency and tenor. To be sure, most of satan's schemes have succeeded because of a general ignorance of the war. Now that Biblio/historical truth has been confirmed, the battle for the soul begins in earnest!

From the very beginning, satan's hatred has raged against God. Again, he wanted to defeat and battle God directly, but lost and was cast down into this realm. In this realm, he cannot fight God. But, he can surely fight against God using the most beloved part of His creation, the "image-bearers." Our foe desires to destroy all of God's creation utterly, but due to God's sovereignty, he has been limited via having only "delegated authority" (God is all-powerful, and while satan has rulership in this realm, he is limited by God's ultimate authority! God's "delegated authority" limits when, where, and how he can do certain things in this realm.) The aforementioned notwithstanding, satan's unfettered hatred and attempts to utterly decimate God's creation did not stop with the woman; his hateful aggressions carried to the second part of the Genesis 3:15 verse, to include the "offspring."

Why must satan's rage also extend to the most innocent? Why must he also target "offspring?" The answer is, the baby is representative of the "essence" of God! Babies are the innocent, beautiful, loving and perfect example and a reminder of human beings as being made in of the "image and likeness" of God. That said, satan has unbounded hate for them! He longs to destroy all babies! As

> *If one side can "choke off" opposing forces, they (most times) win the battle due to limited resources and dwindling personnel and/or supplies*

he targets women for destruction, it is the baby that is his ultimate target since they extend numbers of participants on the battlefield. Babies, each possessing the essence of God, provide satan impetus and motivation to develop deceptions and schemes to eliminate them indiscriminately. They are innocent (not knowing or participating in "good" or "evil"), and therefore constant reminders of God's miracle of life to us. But to satan, babies are viewed as potentially dangerous "enemy combatants" because as they grow, they may come to know and trust God; they have the capacity to become warriors on the battlefield for God ultimately, and this represents an incalculable risk to our foe's battlefield strategies! As with any war planning, our foe feels he must control the battlefield and outcomes by restricting and/or eliminating the number of combatants. Being God's cherished and perfectly hand-formed "image- bearers" is hard enough to contend with, but when coupled with the fact that babies also have the capacity to become warriors for God, satan's motivation and aggressive zeal to eliminate all babies is manifest.

All good battle plans include tactics designed to limit and restrict opposition on the battlefield. If one can control and limit the "theater of war" by limiting personnel/resources on one side vs. the other, the one side with the most fervent fighters on the battlefield can almost assure victory over the side with limited personnel/resources. The best war generals, who have demonstrated the greatest success, have been honored because they employed tactics and strategies that included limiting and restricting supply-lines and personnel. Again, if one side can "choke off" opposing forces, they (most times) win the battle due to limited resources and dwindling personnel and/or supplies. It's easy to see satan's war against women is being waged with this exact tactic and strategy. In the demonic realm, satan uses masterful deceptions to embolden and broaden his "army" (in this case, zealous unwitting "feminists"), and they actually carry out fighting on his side as he veils the fact that their effort actually reinforces his hateful scheme to reduce and utterly destroy women ... via the baby!

Imagine that! Our foe uses humanity to win in his war against humanity. With the backdrop of what's been uncovered thus far about satan's war on God's creation/humanity, using battleground tactics that include targeting women and offspring for destruction, it becomes more clear why some of the most heinous atrocities in all of human history have been expressly targeted at babies. Women have certainly been maligned and horribly abused, but no single demographic has endured anything close to the tactics our foe used to decimate and utterly destroy babies.

Before coming to know the truth about satan's war on women, I used to reflexively experience base revulsion in utter horror when reading of the child sacrifices to Moloch and Baal. The first question that came to my mind was, "How could those parents willingly (and purportedly gleefully) give their children up for such heinous sacrifice and traditions?" These acts were most repulsive and incomprehensible!

The Bible confirms Moloch was an idol god (worshipped as a deity) depicted as a bronze statue. The bronze statue had the face of a bull, multiple chambers, and an opening in the "stomach." The stomach of Molech burned intensely hot and with fury, and this is where children would be placed or thrown in and burned alive (as a child sacrifice); as intensely hot fire would burn and child "sacrifices" offered, the idol god's anger would be assuaged. These were obvious callous attacks on God's creation, and God admonished and rebuked accordingly: Lev 18:21~ "You must not give any of your children to be sacrificed to Moloch, for you must not profane the name of your God. I am the LORD." Lev 20:2-5~ "Then the LORD said to Moses, 'Tell the Israelites, 'Any Israelite or foreigner living in Israel who gives any of his children to Moloch must be put to death. The people of the land are to stone him. And I will set My face against that man and cut him off from his people because by giving his offspring to Moloch, he has defiled My sanctuary and profaned My holy name. And if the people of the land ever hide their eyes and fail to put to death the man who gives one of his children to Moloch, then I will set My face against that man and his family and cut off from their people both him and all who follow him in prostituting themselves with Moloch." God hates all idol worship, but his intense fury was especially evident when it came to Moloch.

God declared there was a war between "the serpent" and the woman and offspring. So it is not hard to imagine the deep anger He felt when His creation was actually working against itself on the side of the eternal enemy who had been cast out of the heavens. Not only was He righteously angered at the people for setting up and sacrificing to idols (before Him), but He also showed no mercy and commanded death upon those that would literally fight and battle for satan by heinously sacrificing the precious children that God had just meticulously assembled in the womb and had given destiny! (Jer 1:5 "Before I formed you in the womb I knew you, and before you were born I set you apart..." Ps 139:13~ "For You formed my inmost being; You knit me together in my mother's womb"). Even after God's anger and admonitions, brazen rebellion and child sacrifices to idol gods continued.

Baal was worshipped as the sun god and storm god. In his book, "Jezebel's war with America," Dr. Michael Brown writes of Baal, "According to Canaanite myth, Baal (whose name means "master, lord") was the son of El, the chief deity (whose name means "god"), and his wife Asherah. Baal was a weather deity, which also meant he was associated with the fertility of the land, while Asherah was a fertility goddess par excellence. Bible teacher Ray Vander Laan notes that Baal is portrayed as a man with the head and horns of a bull...His right hand (sometimes both hands) is raised, and he holds a lightning bolt, signifying both destruction and fertility. As for Asherah, she is portrayed as a nude female, sometimes pregnant, with exaggerated (or multiple) breasts that she holds as a symbol of the fertility. He goes on, "At time of crisis, Baal's followers sacrificed their children, apparently the first born of the community, to gain personal prosperity."[4] Baal worship ceremonies were mostly sensual, and at time's required human sacrifice; again, usually, this was the firstborn child.

When connecting the dots of idol god ceremonies used in ancient child sacrifices, it is quite illuminating! With Moloch, babies/children were rolled down a ramp into a gaping pit filled with fire, thrown into the ferociously hot incinerator of the belly (or stomach, or womb) of the idol, and burned alive in the most grotesque ways. Think of it, satan is literally mocking God with imagery of babies of His creation burning up in the womb! Baal & Asherah sacrifices required sensualities and perverted sex acts as part of the ceremonies. After wanton vile ceremonial acts, babies were sacrificed on the altar of the idol. Think of the mindset and worldview of those who would even consider doing such detestable acts! Consider how the enemy,

---

[4]   *Jezebel's War with America, Michael L. Brown, PhD. Chapt 2, pg 19-20*

satan, seduced, and compelled parents to sacrifice their own first-born children in the most heinous ways. How could satan seduce parents to do this? He cunningly seduced through masterful deceptions that appealed to personal feelings of being part of "progressive" elitists (enlightenment) in ode to the gods. This same cunning modality continues to this very day!

One thing we can count on about our foe, he (satan) is a master deceiver! He deceives by playing on base human frailties and vices, like avarice, hedonism, debauchery and "convenience" (among countless others). In sacrifices to Moloch and Baal, the parents of children wanted "favor" with the gods for rather simple comforts like better weather, abundant crops, more children (imagine that) and etc. Participation in these sacrifices was seen as "enlightened" and "progressive," thus fueling parents' motivations for more advanced social status and a heightened need to accommodate base sensual sensibilities (Baal ceremonies were notably sensual/sexual, as Baal was also seen as a fertility god). Progressive thought leaders were leaders of these tribal communities and used their satan-inspired influence and authority to compel parents to sacrifice their children (Hmmm...does this sound familiar?). It is important to note, just as God uses people to grow and influence His Kingdom in this realm, our foe also precipitates his diabolical warfare in this earthly realm through people. While God is delighted by his creation being "fruitful and multiplying," satan fights wholly against this and attempts to eliminate populations by deceiving people into actually fighting on his side of the battle with schemes designed to reduce or eliminate children purposely. Again, in battleground parlance, eliminating opposition is a consummate battleground tactic, and satan desires to eliminate all of humankind via deceiving the world to the extent it will celebrate an embrace aborting its progeny.

The attack on babies has been persistent, continual and (believe it or not) even increasingly more aggressive over the millenniums. What can possibly be more aggressive and abhorrent than throwing babies into a furnace? Over the centuries, there have actually been many satan-inspired brutal, murderous people with ghoulish appetites and fetishes that fed on suffering and torture of babies! With many in full embrace of demonic delusions, there is never a shortage of those who proudly kill the most innocent under the guise of "service to humanity" and "progressivism."

One of the most notorious satan-inspired persons in history is Josef Mengele. Mengele was one of Hitler's main Nazi captains. He was a German physician and SS captain.[5] "He was the most prominent of a group of Nazi doctors who conducted medical experiments that often caused great harm or death to the prisoners. In November 1943 Mengele became "Chief Camp Physician" of Auschwitz II (Birkenau). Many of those subjected to Mengele's experiments died as a result or were murdered in order to facilitate post-mortem examination." Mengele was a student of eugenics as, like with most of his contemporaries, he was a firm believer in German-race superiority. While he maimed adults in the most heinous ways, Mengele was especially captivated by babies (and especially twin babies); he conducted horrendous child experiments, including taking babies iris' out to simply determine differences in coloration. Unless they were twins, Mengele ordered that all Jewish babies born in Nazi camps to be immediately exterminated. Midwives would deliver the live births, then immediately drown the babies in shallow pales in front of the mothers. Hitler's Nazi camps were camps of unfathomable horrors. "Doctors," like Josef Mengele are perfect examples of our foe's use of humanity as soldiers doing his bidding on his side of the battlefield. This is how he's waging war. Hitler knew, the more Jews proliferated, the greater the risk of losing the battle. Hitler strategically had his Nazi's soldiers to capture them, torture them, and fundamentally eliminate them by controlling all the women and then eliminating their offspring! Again, our foe's war against women is his way to wage war against all God's creation, and he uses the grand strategy of eliminating humanity in an attempt to limit and control God's side of the battlefield. Babies represent progeny and a legacy that satan cannot control, so his only option is to do all he can to eliminate them. Sadly, history and brutal statistics show with these evil tactics, he's been winning...

If you calculate every person killed as a result of the evilest and despotic totalitarian regimes in world history (including Mao's China, Hitler, Stalin, Mussolini, Pol Pot), death totals would be estimated at over 100,000,000 killed. Think about that! Over one hundred million innocent souls mercilessly murdered. According to the New York Times,[6] if you combine that 100 Million souls with the number of deaths from every war

---

[5] *National Museum of Auschwitz-Birkenau*
[6] *New York Time 'What Every Person Should Know about War' July 6, 2003*

that has been fought in human history, you would end up with between 150 million to 1 billion. These numbers are indeed unthinkable and quite staggering. But, those deaths, while horrendous, don't come anywhere near the number of innocent children brazenly killed in the most horrific ways in just the past 50 years! Astonishing! How can it be that the number of babies killed far surpass the number of all human atrocities at the hands of the worst despots, and including all war deaths, from the beginning of time? In a word, abortion! Abortion is the single most lethal weapon our foe uses to wage war against humanity and rage against God. With every baby, God celebrates His new masterpiece; satan then unleashes evils of abortion to virtually spit in God face in an ultimate act of jealous rage. Our foe's boundless rage has had devastating results. According to the World Health Organization (WHO), every year there are an estimated 40-50 million abortions (worldwide). This corresponds to approximately 125,000 abortions per day. In the USA, nearly half of pregnancies are unintended, and four in 10 of these are terminated by abortion; there are over 3,000 abortions per day. Twenty-two percent of all pregnancies in the USA (excluding miscarriages) end in abortion. To be sure, the National Right to Life (NRLC) confirms the total number of abortions since 1973 Supreme Court decision on Roe v. Wade, over 61,628,584 abortions have been performed; think about that, in the U.S. alone over 60 million of God's cherished children have been eliminated via abortion in the in the past 40+ years![7] These statistics are significant because through them we can tangibly discern our foe's hateful determination to undermine women, utterly destroy children, and decimate God's perfect will for humanity.

In this binary war, our collective enemy has unleashed a grandmaster battle plan in his war on women. While God assuredly pronounces, "Behold, children are a heritage from the Lord, the fruit of the womb *is* a reward" ~PS 127:3 (NKJV), satan aggressively pushes his plan of mass elimination of God's "rewards." In sheer numbers, satan's master plan to scatter and decimate the battlefield by eliminating combatants on God's side has been succeeding. His strategy has culminated in the death of 1.5 to 2 billion children being eliminated in just the past 50 years.[8] With up to 2 billion souls prevented from entering the battle in just the

---

[7]   NRLC.org FS01 Abortion fact sheet

[8]   Mas on, Volin and Mosher, Stephen. Earth Day: Life Site News April 21, 2011

> *His strategy has culminated in the death of 1.5 to 2 billion children being eliminated in just the past 50 years.*

last 50 years, it is likely that at least double that amount has been proactively taken off the battlefield in the millennia's preceding. Ironically, since our foe is a master deceiver, he has successfully used women to precipitate and wage his war against their own women. Now, we see millions of women cheer as they gleefully facilitate their own demise and the demise of their progeny. The primary deceptive tool satan has used to malign and disempower women is self-destruction through abortion. What's so telling about the over 1-2 billion abortions that have been conducted is that there was a purposeful action taken to utterly destroy babies in only the most heinous ways.

As compared to any living organism, babies have endured the worst and most heinous acts of elimination. And with satan's brazen war against women and offspring, even as God mandated humanity to "be fruitful and multiply," he has only increased his jealous fervor to utterly devastate the most innocent of God's handiwork. While there have been many notorious demonically inspired people who have fought on satan's battlefield by decimating babies, none have been as diabolically vile and destructive as modern-day abortionists. (Make no mistake abortion/infanticide IS the dividing line on the battlefield, and is a specific and essential tactic used to undermine God and His creation). When you combine body-part dismemberment, with cutting of the spine and sucking out the brains of babies (even after confirming them as "pain-capable"), you can sense our foe's vile hatred being manifested to this very day. His boundless hatred toward babies is magnified when you see State leaders pushing infanticide via delivering the live baby, then later deciding on how to "just make it comfortable" then kill it. To be sure, Virginia's Democrat Governor Ralph Northam believes babies, even after birth, should not be given the same protections that he and all other citizens are afforded.[9] True to form, Democrats declare unborn children are not human and therefore are not entitled to rights. (Remember, this is the exact same rationale and argument Democrats used as they tortured, maimed and lynched Black slaves in the

---

[9] *"Gov. Ralph Northam: 'I Don't have any regrets' About Infanticide Comments"- Grace Carr, The Daily Signal, February 01, 2019*

1800s). The ghoulish ways babies are treated is surely incomprehensible; realistically, our minds can't quite fathom or process the many cruel ways our foe targets babies to be killed to this very day.

Countless atrocities directed at babies seem endless. In Zimbabwe, "newborn babies clog up the sewers in the Capital Harare, because so many are flushed down toilets and flushed into drains-about 20 per week![10]" Think of it, precious babies that God just finished forming are being flushed down toilets and treated worse than trash.

How can it be that so many have been encouraged and motivated to participate on satan's side in his war against women under the auspices of fighting in the war for women and their rights? In eternity past, Lucifer was masterfully deceptive and manipulative, and as an Archangel of worship, he was able to deceive 1/3 of the heavenly hosts to join him and rebel against God. Think about it, they willingly rebelled against the God they served face-to-face! Yet and still, they rebelled! If he can convince angelic hosts to rebel, surely he can manipulate fallen humanity. He is the serpent/ satan in this realm and is relegated to fighting the battle against God by using God's created beings against themselves. With our limited capacity of human cognition, it hard to imagine the level of deception that can be promulgated from " the god of this world." It would be incomprehensible to imagine human beings fighting and warring in alignment with their mortal enemy to (self-eliminate) as a virtue. But here we are, sacrificing children as a virtue may be hard to imagine, but alas, we are experiencing tangible levels of deception that can be seen …and (wittingly or unwittingly) fully experienced!

The unveiling to this point provides the "big reveal" of some inconvenient and indisputable facts. There is no doubt these facts go against preconceived notions and mindsets. Surely, our foe's cunning and manipulation are working in overdrive even now in hopes you find some way to reject the revealed Biblical facts and truth! To hold on to existing mindsets that reject what's been unveiled (to this point) without apology, repentance or regret, you would surely be considered a Bible, history and

---

10 *"Newborn corpses, fetuses found in sewer blockages in Zimbabwe," Associated Press Feb, 17th 2006*

THE WAR ON WOMEN

"science denier." You would have to believe the Bible is false, that it is mere coincidence women continue to be aggressively maligned and abused at increasing levels (and frequency), and that the 2+billion babies that have been slaughtered have not been "targets" of an eternal battle infused with satanic motivations and underpinnings; you would have to believe they are somehow just coincidently and conveniently slaughtered as part of a normal progression of culture and society! If you indeed reject all that's been confirmed thus far, you would have some level of confirmation (within yourself) that you are stricken with a stronghold of the mind, and it prevents logic and prudence. Because of it, you have confirmed our foe has been successful (in your own life) in producing suffering from acute "soul sickness."

Closing Arguments

Children are a primary target and have suffered the most in satan's war against women. Many have participated in undermining God (mostly unwittingly), while holding fast to deceptions of our foe's tactics and strategies unleashed to reduce participants in the cosmic battle via killing babies (by either via sacrifices of old, or via abortion). After considering the truth about the cosmic battle and its respective targets (women and offspring), every individual should be compelled to contemplate, "How will you fight FOR women in satan's war being waged against women?"

CHAPTER 7

"IF I WERE THE DEVIL"....

Opening Statement

The guile and cunning from our foe cannot be overstated;
these are formidable attributes of our foe!
He is the "father of lies" and masterful at all deceptions. When
we consider sheer audacity it takes to beguile individuals to the
extent they take up arms and fight on your side of the battle
as you fight against them, you come to understand satan is a
most formidable foe! In addition, being masterful at lies and
deceptions, the ability to shroud, veil, and conceal his actual
agendas (even if it's "in your face") should confirm the level of
contemptible foe we face.

I have no doubt that even with facts and confirmation presented thus far about satan's war on women, many "people of Faith," "Progressives," "feminists," Leftists, and others are still grappling with how to reconcile the newfound facts about satan's war. They wrestle with how to hold on to a mind-frame that would allow keeping existing perspective without a total collapse of worldview. When we realize that we've been deceived into believing in mere "shadows" of what we thought was a vital cultural cause in fighting for the "war on women," a total collapse of worldview is inevitable; this results in the veritable "veil" being lifted. When the veil is lifted, we can sense this war is not trivial. It's spiritual! Truly, the antidote to an aggressive and determined evil foe is spiritual. Unbeknownst to the casual reader, this war and battle has taken us to the "edge of our natural understanding (and senses)," and we are now entering the zone of very real "Spiritual warfare." This is what precipitates change in mindset.

One of the best ways to move existing mindsets into new frames of reference, and ultimately to the point of acceptance, is through demonstration of powerful (yet prescient) analogies of the cosmic battle. Scholar and theologian, C.S Lewis, taught us this when he used his classic masterpiece The Screwtape Letters, to portray human life from the perspective of a demon. This powerful portrayal gives a somewhat comedic portrayal of temptation, deception, and the myriad tactics of the demonic realm. This masterpiece is viewed as a very powerful way to demonstrate the moment-to-moment battles we face in the war against the demonic realm.

In 1965, famous radio broadcaster Paul Harvey, provided a powerfully prescient and prophetic analogy, "If I Were the Devil." In this speech, Harvey uses his knowledge of satan and his tactics, to convey how he (satan) would use culture and society to destroy and undermine collective humanity. He appropriately, but satirically, confirmed methods of deception satan would use in order to control and undermine societies. "If I were The Devil" provides a window of a powerful, easily consumable analogy...Or, is it reality? The following is Paul Harvey's "If I were The Devil":

If I were the Devil, if I were the Prince of Darkness, I'd want to engulf the whole world in darkness and I would have a third of its real estate and four-fifths of its population, but I wouldn't be happy until I had seized the ripest apple on the tree, thee.

So, I would set about however necessary to take over the United States. I'd subvert the churches first. I'd begin with a campaign of whispers. With the wisdom of a serpent, I would whisper to you as I whispered to Eve: "Do as you please."

To the young, I would whisper that the Bible is a myth. I would convince them that man created God instead of the other way around. I would confide that what is bad is good and what is good is "square." And the old, I would teach to pray after me: "Our Father which art in Washington."

And then I'd get organized. I'd educate authors in how to make lurid literature exciting so that anything else would appear dull and uninteresting. I'd make TV look worse than movies and then make movies look worse than TV in a vicious cycle that just gets worse and worse. I'd peddle narcotics to whomever [sic] I could. I'd sell alcohol to ladies and gentlemen of distinction. I'd tranquilize the rest with pills.

If I were the Devil, I'd soon have families at war with themselves, churches at war with themselves, and nations at war with themselves, until each in its turn was consumed. And with promises of higher ratings, I'd have mesmerizing media fanning the flames.

If I were the Devil, I would encourage schools to refine young intellects but neglect to discipline emotions; just let those run wild until, before you knew it, you'd have to have drug-sniffing dogs and metal detectors at every schoolhouse door. Within a decade, I'd have prisons overflowing. I'd have judges promoting pornography. Soon I could evict God from the courthouse, and then from the schoolhouse, and then from the houses of Congress. And in His own churches I would substitute psychology for religion and deify science. I would lure priests and pastors into misusing boys and girls and church money. If I were the Devil, I'd make the symbol of Easter an egg and the symbol of Christmas a bottle.

If I were the Devil, I would take from those who have and give to those who wanted, until I had killed the incentive of the ambitious. And what will you bet I couldn't get whole states to promote gambling as the way to get rich. I would caution against extremes in hard work, in patriotism, in moral conduct. I would convince the young that marriage is old-fashioned, that swinging is more fun, that what you see on TV is the way to be and thus I could undress you in public and I could lure you into bed with diseases for which there is no cure.

In other words, if I were the devil, I'd just keep right on doing what he's doing."

This was a speech given over 50 years ago! Wow…Paul Harvey was indeed prescient and prophetic! His exposition helps make rather abstract occurrences that are hard to measure moment-to-moment much more discernable and concrete. Thinking deeply and musing (from a diabolical perspective) about what is happening in society, provides is with a somewhat easier way to discern tactics and strategies our foe is using to destroy humanity.

If one were to further expound on Paul Harvey's profound exposition of 50 years ago to include many of the latest forms of socio/structural changes within culture and society, what would the "If I Were the Devil" speech sound like today? In consideration of satan's war on women and her offspring, and reflecting on current socio/cultural trends, here is my attempt at a current rendition of "If I Were the Devil":

If I were the devil, I would masterfully deceive "the masses" into believing I don't exist! If they believe I don't exist, they will never know of my war on women and will be willing vessels to carry out my battle-plans to destroy God's creation while destroying themselves.

If I were the devil, I would shroud/veil hearts and minds with negative emotions (especially emotions of grievance and "offense"), instead of relying on logic and prudence! I would deceive people into being quickly triggered toward anger, hatred and outrage; this will keep "the masses" angry and projecting outward (targeting their personal anger toward others) thereby making introspection impossible, and incapable of discerning how they're actively being used to wage my war against God and his creation.

If I were the devil, I would lie and manipulate all into believing God is not active today in the affairs of men, therefore, waiting for Him to mete out righteous recompense and justice, is fool-hearted and not progressive or enlightened. I'd get them to believe "justice" (today) can only be achieved by force! March & rally! Agitate! Demand! Reparations!

If I were the devil, I'd deceive Churches into believing "race disparities," "Social Justice" and "taking care of the poor" should take primacy over the Bible and spreading the Gospel of the Kingdom. This way, the Church becomes complacent, anemic, and impotent, while I deviously spread new gospels surrounding social activism (actual anathemas to God).

If I were the devil, the primary weapon I would use to win in my war on women is the woman! As a "masterstroke" of genius, I would actually use women to wage my war against themselves; most importantly, I'd deceive her (using "convenience" and resentment) to willingly eliminate her own offspring! I'd make them feel virtuous as they rail against "patriarchy" and objectification, while willfully proffering vulgar, immodest objectification onto themselves. Using God's own creation to destroy themselves by bowing to me and waging my war, is my ultimate slap to God's face!

I would deceive Churches into believing "Separation of Church and State" means they should reject civic engagement!

If I were the devil, I would wholly deceive "intellectual elites" ("media," academia, politicians) into fighting my battle against God and His creation, via undermining women by way of killing off their offspring (via abortion); I'd use abortion as a "progressive" enlightened virtue! "Intellectuals" are excellent instruments to proliferate mass deception.

If I were the devil, I would deceive Churches into believing "Separation of Church and State" means they should reject civic engagement! This prevents them from voting and electing people of their mindset; this allows my stronghold on culture to expand as the Church sits idly by. While they claim God in their hearts, I will have unfettered access to their souls (mind, will, and emotions), and use their silence as complicity as I wage my war on women.

If I were the devil, I would deceive the masses by veiling hearts and minds with an intense focus on "racial issues" as the fundamental grievance to overcome. By focusing them on "race," it'll override logic, reason, Faith/religion, traditions, and allow unfettered access to human frailties as I wage my war against God and His creation.

If I were the devil, I would use "gender dysphoria" to confuse and undermine God's creation and prevent them from being "fruitful and multiplying." I'd use schools to sexualize and confuse children starting in kindergarten. Ultimately, through their early sexualization and confusion, many will grow frustrated and self-eliminate (suicide); the cosmic battlefield will grow resentful, confused, and hateful toward God because of their dysphoria...God's battlefield will ultimately be reduced and destroyed.

If I were the devil, I would deceive "people of Faith" into actually battling on my side of the war against God and humanity by convincing them they could still be "good Christians" while also embracing "radical feminism," voting for pro-abortion candidates, and tacitly supporting abortion! They'll be so deluded, they'll actually march on my side of the battle, help me precipitate undermining the "woman and her offspring," and virtually spit in the face of their creator (Ha! This is my delicious irony!)

In the end, If I were the devil, I would just keep doing what I'm doing...I'm winning the war, and I'm unstoppable!

It should be becoming clearer how our chief foe and the committed enemy uses powerful deceptions to actually enlist and motivate humanity in his war against God and humanity! While it's obviously "circular insanity," it is a very powerful and clever strategy that is working on all tactical levels. Our foe has women actually warring to undermine themselves in his war on women, he has "people of Faith" helping him win in a war against the very God they commit their lives to, he has deceived scholarly "intellectuals" into embracing illogical mindsets in rejection of scientific/biological fact about when life begins and biology surrounding only two genders (male and female), and he has "mothers" willing to kill their own children (mostly out of convenience) as willing participants in his war against women and offspring!

Only a continuous and aggressive campaign of mass deception can move people to embrace diabolical "strongholds" and entrenched mindsets that actually facilitate their own demise. God wants to lift us out of demonic deceptions by lifting the veil so we can see, discern, and wholly commit to His side of the war for the women and offspring.

With the renewed capacity to observe the actual war and renewed fortitude to allow serious introspection, we can reject our foe's aggressive campaigns of deception. This is a critical step for turning the tide in the war...

Closing Argument

The use of allegories is a good way to make the battle with our chief foe tangible and "perceptible." His principal tactic is endless lies and deceit, and his strategies reach far into the arena of ideologies, social movements, and culture. Once he deceives mass numbers of individuals, he produces deceptive mass ideologies, and then popularizes social movements, which then produces cultural chaos! Unmasking satan's deceptions is critical to turning the tide in his war...

CHAPTER 8

WEAPON OF MASS DECEPTION: FROM "DARK SHADOWS" TO ENTRENCHED MINDSETS

Opening Statement

Satan's use of deceptions are so keen, he can take our most fleeting passing thoughts like, "I wonder, what it would be like to be a girl," to a demand that "I am a girl and you better recognize me as such!" Our foe's ability to take our individual (and otherwise preposterous) "shadows of thought," to then turn into actual ideologies that transform into social movements that shape culture, is insidious "genius." Undermining humanity becomes much easier using such strategies. His side of battle becomes much easier as mindsets on the opposing side of the cosmic battlefield are left deranged and/or demoralized...

Since our foe wages a persistent war against the human mind and soul, a look inward validates our life stance is a step toward vigilant introspection. A serious and continual looking inward is what constitutes introspection. Through introspection, God provides us the capacity to interrogate our thoughts and feelings so that we may gain the ability of observe and follow common sense and hold to personal values and truth. Our foe is on the other end of the spectrum. He is the same cunning liar he was in the garden of Eden, and to this very day, euphemistically slithers around seeking to deceive us in the exact same way he did in Eden. With his endgame focused on winning the battle against God and humanity, satan's deceptions are his most powerfully pivotal tools. With such a committed foe, only spending time in prayerful introspection can forestall his endless assaults on our mind.

Right now, our mind should be confirming that if we do *anything* that harms women and babies/children, we are actually working for and battling on the side of our eternal foe. That fact notwithstanding, many will no doubt deceive themselves via the embrace of sheer delusions, so they can hold on to existing mindsets. Only a master liar and deceiver can blind the minds of masses of humanity for millennia's while shrouding their minds to not fully comprehend ramifications of the first declared war instantiated against all humankind (in the Garden of Eden). Since that day in the garden, he's been waging war with vigor and power while humanity has been blinded and therefore helping precipitate its own demise. With all that's been uncovered about his ability to deceive humanity into effectively waging war against God, he's been masterful at creating strongholds of entrenched mindsets in his favor.

If we are truthful with ourselves, we would agree that at some point in our lives, we've been deceived by our foe's machinations into participating in his war against us. Based on his lies, deceptions, and raw emotions, most have been gripped and swept into entrenched mindsets. Proliferations of entrenched diabolical mindsets are his chief tool for deception. You know there's an entrenched mindset and stronghold when people stridently believe they are actually helping in the "war on women" while heralding as enlightened and progressive, the killing of her offspring. You know there is a stronghold when, even after God ordains that humankind should "be fruitful and multiply," women completely eschew and reject childbearing in deference to talking points asserting more population is a "hazard to climate change." You know there's a mindset stronghold when women proclaim they hate being "objectified," while they gleefully participate in "women's marches" wearing vile and grotesque vagina hats, anatomically explicit vagina costumes and other wholly immodest images that only help them undermine and objectify themselves as sex objects! They've now even gone as far as to embrace witchcraft, incantations and demonism openly. Journalist Jim Hoft shares his observations as follows, "In case you missed it, the Women's March Twitter account is now advocating 'casting spells' as a means of 'fighting the patriarchy.' The new Left has no tolerance for Christianity – but they love their witchcraft! It's disturbing that witchcraft and Satanism have been normalized to the point where mainstream political organizations are openly advocating it.[11] Brazenly casting demonic spells and incantations is a most telling data point for those still not convinced of the level of demonism embraced via "feminists" and supporters of the women's marches. Don't ignore the signs; take note! Diabolical mindsets are taking hold of culture and society.

You know there's an embrace of entrenched diabolical mindset when large percentages of Christians (and even Pastors/Clergy) tacitly endorse abortion, "radical feminism," and give primacy to an unholy embrace of racial animus toward others! All of these are indicative of unholy worldviews and are strategically used by satan in the war against God and humanity. With these few examples of entrenched diabolical mindsets, the more important issue to understand is how satan popularizes the embrace of diabolical mindsets.

Preying on base human frailties and insecurities are powerful ways satan uses to dislodge and unmoor humanity from morality and objective truth. Based on his experience with Eve in the garden, he knows people can be greatly influenced by those they deem as "brilliant and enlightened." If influencers are cunning like the serpent in the garden, and are positioned to prey on base frailties (like loneliness, insecurities, delusions of grandeur, etc.), they can easily manipulate others in order to unmoor people from foundational truths; ultimately, a change in worldview occurs.

There have been many who have been used to transform worldviews as they've been heralded as "intellectual," "enlightened", and "progressive"; ultimately, they were demonic "tools" being used to corrupt societies and proliferate satan's war against humanity. From miscreants (like the pharaohs and Jezebel in Biblical times), to authoritarian despots (like

---

[11] *Jim hoft, Gateway Pundit November 10, 2019*

Hitler, Mao, Stalin and etc. during periods of World Wars), to modern-day icons (like Margret Sanger, Saul Alinsky, and James Cone), there is a clear, unmistakable history of nefarious demonism precipitated by people with notable following. (Note: This is not an assessment of their eternal disposition. In this context, I am only referring to how these people were used by satan to alter morality and shift worldviews in his war against God and humanity)

In the case of the pharaohs and Jezebel, people worshiped them due to raw power, beauty and seduction; these attributes veiled their inherent evil as they led people to abandon their roots, and worship idol gods and sacrifice babies/children. Authoritarian despots (Hitler, Mao, Stalin, etc.) used "populism" and "nationalism," promises of utopia, personal charisma, "Social Justice" and totalitarian power to influence the masses into tacitly participating in war, mass murders, and genocide. Walter E. Williams, columnist for The Daily Signal and a professor of economics at George Mason University poignantly sums it up this way, "According to professor R.J. Rummel's research in 'Death by Government,' from 1917 until its collapse, the Soviet Union murdered or caused the death of 61 million people, mostly its own citizens. From 1949 to 1976, Mao's communist regime was responsible for the death of as many as 76 million Chinese citizens. Today's leftists, socialists, and progressives would bristle at the suggestion that their agenda differs little from that of past tyrants. They should keep in mind that the origins of the unspeakable horrors of Nazism, Stalinism, and Maoism did not begin in the '20s, '30s, and '40s. Those horrors were simply the result of a long evolution of ideas leading to a consolidation of power in the central government in the quest for "social justice."

Modern-day cultural icons like Margret Sanger (Planned Parenthood Founder who ushered in radical feminism), Saul Alinsky (radical Marxist who ushered in diabolical forms of "community organizing") and James Cone ("theologian" who ushered Churches into embracing "Black Liberation theology") were used to encourage and enshrine abortion, agitate and sow discord throughout all factions of society, and to illuminate "race" and Marxism as supreme over and above the Gospel of the Kingdom (respectively). These few random individuals have produced profound diabolical effects on culture and society under the guise of "Social Justice." While their personal mindsets were viewed as "radical" and "out there" ("mere shadows") when they started, by their lives, they were enshrined as icons and pioneers of major social movements.

While it may seem hard to believe that a few random individuals have had such a profound impact on world history and humanity (in general), it should be noted that "worldview" is not always scrutinized by logic, reason and prudence. It can be very heavily influenced by momentum and momentous occasions. As such, satan seeks to use and manipulate individuals that carry immense power and influence and with just a slight "tweak" and perversion of truth (like, "the baby is just a mass of cells," and "Jesus was Socialist"), he builds out new movements that are mere "shadows" of truth (but in actuality, huge lies bringing severe consequences nevertheless). In the end, nefarious movements gain momentum via inertia as they burgeon and cascade, wholly expanding the battlefield for our foe while significantly reducing the participants on God's side of the battle. A common denominator of all of the prior mentioned miscreants is they worked diligently to increase and herald "state power"; they were diligent about encouraging and esteeming "statism," which is when significant centralized control is given to the State (government) to oversee all social and economic affairs. Why would statist schemes and machinations be an important element encouraged and used by our foe? With statism, satan can achieve better and more predictable control of the battlefield! He can posit "big government" as all-powerful and in need of reverence; he can juxtapose big government you can see and experience as the "real god!" Federalist, Fisher Ames, in an essay during the early years of the Republic stated, "In any age, the so-called progressives treat politics as their religion. Their holy mission is to use the coercive power of the State to remake man and society in their own image, according to an abstract idea of perfection. Whatever means they use are therefore justified because, by definition, they are virtuous people pursing a deific end. They are willing to use any means necessary to gain a momentary advantage in achieving their end, regardless of collateral consequences and the systemic implications. They never ask whether the actions they take could be justified as a general rule of conduct, equally applicable to all sides."

Tactically speaking, the significance of an all- powerful "state" means by simply using cunning to manipulate a few cloistered "masterminds," satan can potentially control large swaths of the cosmic battlefield. As he posits maladies like atheism into hearts and minds of governmental overseers/masterminds of totalitarian mindset, our foe can wreak havoc on all of humanity. Global "central planners" can usher in a permanent tilt the war in his favor (even though he ultimately loses, he will seemingly control the battle with tactical advantage).

> *...the significance of an all-powerful "state" means by simply using cunning to manipulate a few cloistered "masterminds," satan can potentially control large swaths of the cosmic*

For example, if "globalism"/"One World Government"/"New World Order" were ever wholly adopted and the U.N controlled (or authoritatively influenced) the world, satan only need to manipulate and deceive some few of the key central planners into adopting strict population controls. This would result in billions of babies being wiped out and kept off the battlefield. This is not far-fetched! Several past U.S. Presidents were actually keen on pursuing globalism. This is why we must reject all efforts masterminds use to encourage ceding of personal liberties and freedoms over to overarching centralized government entities; insisting on maintaining all personal freedoms are Godly response to governments while empowering a "nanny-state" in hopes of having every need taken care of, is fundamental to a pagan-state (i.e. demonic).

Make no mistake, there is a clear, quite definitive connection between totalitarian central planners and the assault on women and offspring. They work hand-in-hand in our foe's schemes to wage war on women. Author William Dodd states, "The common thread that unites the social engineers and the implementers who followed is atheism. And the state-supported practice that has become Socialism's identifying mark is abortion. For those who promote and operate the abortion industry, with no belief in God and or in an afterlife, accepting the notion that abortion does no harm to anyone is understandably easy. There have been over 1.5 billion abortions worldwide since 1980. So an ironic flaw of this atheistic scheme has emerged: *the socialist emancipation of mankind from God is facilitating part of mankind's own destruction.*"[12] (Emphasis added).

Dan Smithwick of the Nehemiah Institute argues that "it is a tyrannical worldview called by various names such as neo-Marxism, transitional Marxism, transformational Marxism, and cultural Marxism. This atheistic worldview is pervasive in our homes, in many churches, in almost all media, in K-20 education, in business and the local, state and national civil governments. It is not politics but effects politics in a very profound way; centralized state government is one of its primary idols. It impacts our culture, including the family, church, state, community, and commerce. It's a full- fledged worldview that constitutes a vicious spiritual war that few believers have been prepared to fight." Fortunately, with our current President, we have someone who is prepared to fight. Based on his Presidency, we have temporary reprieve away from Globalist statist notions. But make no mistake, the vulnerabilities and assault on the woman and her offspring will continue via schemes to use centralized government powers until there are more exposure and the ability for us to "connect the dots" to this opaque aspect of the cosmic battle.

Again, we can only begin to change the landscape and trajectory of the cosmic battle through purposeful introspection and a decidedly prudent approach as to how we should logically embrace worldviews. This is quite possible, but only after we begin to comprehend the strategic significance and influence of social "movements" and their influencers as they look to purposely shape/remake humankind in satan's demonic image.

With what has been revealed about our foe's war on women, it is illogical and untenable for self-described "champions" for women and advocates (in general) to maintain their priorities on our foe's side of the battlefield. "People of Faith" are at the same untenable crossroads; this is the time and day of "choosing"...Based on the Bible and professions of Faith, choose well!

---

[12] *American Th inker, October 7, 2019 Socialism, Atheism, and Abortion By William Dodd*

Closing arguments

Our chief foe conducts his most nefarious works in the shadows. He wants/needs to remain veiled, so he uses "fleeting thoughts and shadows" to generate ideas, which generate ideologies, which generate social movements, which generates culture. Once the culture is changed to the extent it eschews liberty and freedom in deference to the centralized power of governments, demonically inspired cultural transformation will have been dutifully shifted in his favor. If masterminds who can control societies are centralized, all of satan's efforts to manipulate minds can be streamlined and centralized, but he's not lazy! To the contrary, his zeal is to control large swaths of the cosmic battlefield quickly, and control of centralized governments helps maximize his effort!

CHAPTER 9

MUSEFUL MOVEMENTS: THE FOE'S DOOR TO MASS SOCIAL CHAOS!

Opening Statement

Ideology begets personal involvement, personal involvement begets participating in movements (or cause), and movements begets socio/cultural change. Our foe's tactical weapons in his battle against women are the many forms of lies and deceit, and his strategic weapon is culture! Culture can have a profound and sometimes immediate effect on societies; in lieu of slow, incremental, evolutionary changes that can take decades, our foe uses culture to agitate the masses and bring about rapid (albeit diabolical) changes. A "cacophony" of chaotic social movements have emerged, and while they purport differing missions, they ironically have tremendous unity and march in "lock-step." Most who participate in the rejiggering of society through culture, have subjected themselves to social movements and are unwitting tools of nefarious movements wholly committed in our foe's battle in his war on women.

In the earthly realm, satan uses people to execute his fight against God and humanity. Through calculated strategy, our foe tries to attack and manipulate us at the level of personal ideology, then looks to leverage or base emotions and sensitivities to drive us into movements. Satan relies on the fact that significant percentages of humanity are inclined (mostly unwittingly) to create and/or join social "movements"; his goal is to present ideas and schemes via mass social movements that ultimately help extend his diabolical battlefield progression.

Human frailties are finicky. Many have joined movements due to basic human frailties that put a premium on the need to belong to the "collective" and out having sense of "community" even if the respective movement seems paradoxical (or present inconvenient conflicts) with personal values. People just long to belong, therefore many are keen to defocus on base personal values, while launching into and embracing mass social movements as a means toward feeling, that they are contributing to an overarching social good. Since many movements are designed to tap into base emotions ranging from loneliness, detachment, repression, agitation (and countless other emotions) as justification and leverage for action, most movements are embraced without much thought about whether there's logical coherence to an individuals' personal values (or even common sense). Often, and without much thought or hesitation, movements are embraced as a convenient social construct that helps alleviate some form of personal suffering. Alleviating personal needs through a connection with movements is the door our foe uses to launch schemes that actually undermine. His diabolical deeds precipitated by social movements are indeed compelling.

Prior to the 1960s, social movements were largely opportunistic and somewhat disjointed. During the Civil Rights Movement, however, they became structurally coherent and powerful. Movements became even more holistic and sustainable after a notorious Community organizer Saul Alinsky provided a strategic blueprint for social movements in a book called in Rules for Radicals (1971). Alinsky was a notable social malcontent and devious miscreant, but still garnered a huge following that persists to this very day. Even after giving an acknowledgment and dedication of his works to Lucifer in the front pages of his book, he's been lauded by Presidents and Heads of State (B. Obama and H. Clinton are self-professed Alinsky disciples[13],[14])! While Alinsky was a self-professed demoniac, some of the most influential people on the planet follow his blueprint as a virtual "bible" for building movements and changing culture. To be sure, Alinsky's dedication page reads as follows:

Lest we forget at least an over-the-shoulder acknowledgement to the very first radical: from all our legends, mythology and history (and who is to know where mythology leaves off and history begins--or which is which), the first radical known to man who rebelled against the establishment and did it so effectively that he at least won his own kingdom-Lucifer.[15]

It's clear Alinsky had dark motives and allegiances with the demonic realm, yet his legacy is heralded and persists to this day. In his book "How Evil Works," author David Kupelian wrote Obama proclaimed, "Alinsky's community organizing rules were seared into my brain." Kupelian chronicles Alinsky's work as "the general public, must be made to feel intimidated, upset, frustrated, and hopeless. Alinsky explains: Any revolutionary change must be preceded by a passive, affirmative, non-challenging attitude toward change among the mass of our people. They must feel so frustrated, so defeated, so lost, so fruitless in the prevailing system that they are willing to let go of the past and change the future. This acceptance is the reformation essential to any revolution.[16] (emphasis added). Other notable Saul Alinsky quotes from his book, "Rules for Radicals" are: "The first step in community organization is community disorganization. The disruption of the present organization is the first step ...The organizer must first rub raw the resentments of the people of the community; fan the latent hostilities of many of the people to the point of overt expression ...Search out controversy and issues, rather than avoid them, for unless there is controversy people are not concerned enough to act ...The organizer's first job is to create the issues or problems ...An organizer must stir up dissatisfaction and discontent ... The organizer ...

[13]   *Washington Examiner, Matt Peterson, Feb 06, 2012 "Study Saul Alinsky to understand Barack Obama."*
[14]   *Washington Examiner, Roger Kimball, Sept 18, 2016 "Want to understand Hillary Clinton? Read Saul Alinsky"*
[15]   *Saul Alinsky, Rules For Radicals: A Practical Prime r For Realistic Radicals (New York: Random House 1971)- Dedication page*
[16]   *David Kupelian, How Evil Works- 1st Threshold Editions hardcover Pg. 240*

polarizes the issue ...The organizer helps to lead his forces into conflict ... The real arena is corrupt and bloody... In war the end justifies almost any means."

Alinsky's synopsis perfectly underscores how his diabolically inspired strategies are used to undermine existing mindsets and alter worldviews. Since his tactics are entirely designed to precipitate agitation, resentments, and an undue emphasis on "struggle," moral values and common sense should dictate his works must be wholly rejected; but alas, he's cheered as a "Progressive" champion. In addition to Alinsky dedicating his book to lucifer, his entire methodology is designed to foment base emotions of conflict and resentment in order to proffer hatred. Based on his "fruit" alone, there no doubt Alinsky was a tool used by satan, and his legacy and tactics are used to this very day to wage satan's war against women and offspring. To be sure, Proverbs 6:19 remind us: "The Lord hates ... a person who stirs up conflict in the community." (NIV)

It should be noted that as Alinskyite agitators attempt to manipulate in order to change mindsets and worldviews, they'll only succeed if (as Alinsky asserts) "they (the masses) are willing to let go of the past and change the future. This acceptance is the reformation essential to any revolution." This means if we hold fast to our logic, prudence, and Biblical traditions, we gain the capacity to reject joining diabolical social movements and forestall strategic attacks on a personal worldview that undermine God. Today, however, our culture and society are not so thoughtful and perceptive.

Both Hillary Clinton and Barack H. Obama have gleefully accepted Planned Parenthood Awards and honored Margret Sanger (Planned Parenthood Founder) as a quintessential American hero and "women's rights pioneer."[17] That notwithstanding, an accurate view of Sanger's record and account is what provides undisputed truth as to the depth of her delusions and her contorted and contrived heart full of hatred. Some

---

[17] *Sec. Clinton Stands By Her Praise of Eugenicist Margaret Sanger by Kevin Vance| Washington Examiner, April 15, 2009*
Obama Honors Gloria Steinem, Margret Sanger and Planned Parenthood, William Sullivan, Red State February 16, 2012

of Sanger's despicable acts include her actively participating as a keynote speaker for the women's KKK rallies. Sanger was a frequent honored guest at Democrat-led KKK events and ceremonies. While Democrats are still applauding Sanger for being a thought leader and trendsetter, a review of some of her direct quotes actually provides a better gauge of the kind of person she was. Some of Sanger's direct quotes are summarized in the following: "…we are paying for and even submitting to the dictates of an ever-increasing, unceasingly spawning class of human beings who never should have been born at all"- Margret Sanger, "Pivot of Civilization" "The most merciful thing that a large family does to one of its members is to kill it"- Margaret Sanger. "We don't want the word to get out that we want to exterminate the Negro population"- Margaret Sanger. "The purpose of birth control was 'to create a race of thoroughbreds'…"Birth control must ultimately lead to a cleaner race"….- Margaret Sanger, Birth Control Review. "…human weeds," "…reckless breeders," "…unfit," "…feeble- minded" and "…undesirables"- All terms Sanger used to describe and characterize Blacks (and Hispanics) " more children from the fit, less from the unfit—that is the chief aim of birth control"- Sanger. "Blacks and Jews are a menace to the race…We must prevent multiplication of this bad stock…." Sanger. There are much more blatantly horribly evil quotes from Sanger, but they are far too many to mention. Planned Parenthood, as an appendage of feminism, is indicative of influence garnered through socio/cultural movements. From Sanger's diabolical exploits, Roe V. Wade was decided via the Supreme Court, and our society has been permanently transformed (especially considering the 50+ million babies killed since Roe V. Wade).

Because Biblical traditions are usually the hardest foundation to let go, we have seen many theologians who (no doubt) started with great intentions to help the poor and marginalized, now being used as pawns of the satanic realm to purposely target and undermine foundational Biblical beliefs; after amassing great influence within "religious circles," notable figures have infused their personal zeal into theological mindsets, and now present "another gospel." James Cone is one example of a theologian who still has great influence even though he pivoted away from specific Gospel truths, to more stridently embrace theology concerned foremost with race. To be sure, Cone once passionately asserted, "if God is white, Kill God!"

To Cone and his adherents, "race" is preeminent and must be focused on and dealt with before any serious commitment to the written Word of God. To him, God's messages about love and unity (expressed through Jesus) were tripe, especially while Blacks were living with considerable socio/historical disparities (like slavery, race conflicts, oppression and etc.). Based on his writing and works that help borne Black Liberation Theology, Cone felt Blacks (alone) were God's chosen, and "salvation" (all associated eternal "goodness") comes to and through the Black race. Black Liberation Theology (BLT) cleverly uses just enough of the Bible to give it a modicum of credibility, while also focusing on race and conflict as a conduit to power, thus undermining its Biblical authority and authenticity. (Surely, our sovereign and all-powerful God can deliver us from whatever the grievances or conflict; our Bible, not BLT, is our source of truth and promise of deliverance. But based on Cone's assertions, "racial issues" take primacy over the Gospel). While Cone artfully used and attempted to make the Bible an instrument of "race," by extreme contrast, the Bible is actually the wholly Holy instrument of grace. BLT is seductive to those who somehow believe (as Cone did) that God is at times impotent, restricted, unjust and to slow in His divine deliberations; regrettably, there are many who believe this, and are willing to embrace radical undermining of Biblical foundations as well as antithetical Marxist tenants as proof. To be sure, Cones' theology has been recently appended to include Critical Race Theory (CRT).

> *While Cone artfully used and attempted to make the Bible an instrument of "race," by extreme contrast, the Bible is actually the wholly Holy instrument of grace.*

"According to the UCLA School of Public Affairs: "CRT recognizes that racism is engrained in the fabric and system of the American society. The individual racist need not exist to note that institutional racism is pervasive in the dominant culture. This is the analytical lens that CRT uses in examining existing power structures. CRT identifies that these power structures are based on white privilege and white supremacy, which perpetuates the marginalization of people of color. CRT is one of the principal motivators that have people now proclaim "racism" is about power, and is exclusively a white problem. When following this mindset to its next logical conclusion, you would have to say, in order to end racism, all excising power structures must change—a polite way of saying revolution. CRT justifies all affirmative action, reparations, and "hate speech" legislation. All are revolutionary tools derived from Marxism.[18]

Author and filmmaker Trevor Loudon has spent multiple decades researching the radical Left/Leftism and Marxism, and confirms, "There is zero doubt that James Cone was a Marxist. In 1980, the Democratic Socialists of America published an essay by Cone titled 'The Black Church and Marxism: What Do They Have to Say to Each Other?' Louden concludes, "Christianity is based entirely around the individual and his or her relationship with God. It is the individual who may be saved through faith in Jesus Christ, not the collective." Further, Loudon says, "How can a collectivist philosophy that emphasizes racial division above all else and despises all manifestations of individual liberty have anything to offer Christianity? The answer is simple: It doesn't. CRT is a Marxist technique used to divide society into antagonistic racial groups that can be manipulated to create chaos and revolution."[19]Amen! Loudon is spot on!

While some will seek to no doubt trivialize the distinctions between the Gospel of Christ and Liberation Theology, the contrast between the two is quite stark. On the one hand, there is a broken, contrite, and humble ask of the Savior for forgiveness of base human iniquities. On the other, there is a (euphemistically) proud beating of the chest and demanding of recompense for grievances. In other words, one kneels in asking forgiveness and then commits to submission and trust to Lordship of Christ in order to take away sins/guilt/shame, while the other rejects Lordship and instead places demands and responsibility on others to divine recompense by way of guilt and shame. Black Liberation is a perfect example of "another

[18] Trevor Loudon, Marxist "Critical Race theory' Infiltrates Churches, the culture" The Epoch Times , Aug 8, 2019
[19] Trevor Loudon, Marxist "Critical Race theory' Infiltrates Churches, the culture." The Epoch Times , Aug 8, 2019

gospel" that Apostle Paul warned about in Galatians 1:6-9 (NIV) "I am astonished that you are so quickly deserting the one who called you to live in the grace of Christ and are turning to a different gospel—[7] which is really no gospel at all. Evidently, some people are throwing you into confusion and are trying to pervert the gospel of Christ. [8] But even if we or an angel from heaven should preach a gospel other than the one we preached to you, let them be under God's curse! [9] As we have already said, so now I say again: If anybody is preaching to you a gospel other than what you accepted, let them be under God's curse! Sadly, many (including major religious denominations/Churches) have accepted BLT/ CRT gospel, and due to their zeal for this movement, they are living under a self-inflicted curse!

It is abundantly clear worldwide societal change can occur with just a few influential people. It is notable that there is a thread of common denominators that join these people in a shared battle. Even though these individuals were born in different places and times, the 3 individuals overviewed (Sanger, Alinsky, and Cone) had some common "threads." The most compelling threads as it relates to satan's war are: 1. They gained momentum and following in their respective movements by infusing and agitating anger, hatred, and resentment 2. While asserting "feminism" and "Progressivism," they are stridently committed to satan's side of battle by encouraging and pushing abortion. 3. They all pushed for massive radical social change that undermines God and the Bible!

As he wages war against God and humanity, satan masterfully uses charismatic influencers to proliferate socio/cultural movements designed to dislodge traditions and change mindsets. For example, noted strident support for Margret Sanger/Planned Parenthood, coupled with a penchant for demonic witchcraft, confirms radical "feminist/Women's March participants embrace of racism and demonism. If we're sincere, the only way to rationally reconcile actions and behaviors of these groups into a coherent understanding is to conclude, irrespective of their pabulum, their mindsets have rejected norms and traditions and are now inspired by our foe to be racist and demonic (as they aggressively set out to utterly destroy women and offspring)!

A healthy vigilance and circumspection is the best way to prevent the undermining of a personal commitment to battle on God's side in the real fight for women and her offspring.

Closing Argument

We have a pernicious foe who's constantly on the prowl seeking whom he may devour. His insatiable "appetite" is especially attuned to devouring women and offspring (babies), and as such, uses social movements and revolutionaries in an attempt to unmoor us from our principles, values, and common sense! Even if one is not inclined to believe in the Bible, God, or satan, common sense should dictate the attacks on women and offspring are not just part of a normal evolutionary pattern for world societies; due to sheer magnitude of the focused devastation, and intentional acts to destroy women and children, common sense dictates it has to be part of an overarching cosmic battle and strategy! It's time to "wake up!

CHAPTER 10

INTERSECTIONAL MADNESS: THE FOE'S BOUNTIFUL HARVEST OF MASS SOCIAL CHAOS

Opening Statement

Whether we are religious or irreligious, everyone has a worldview. If we have healthy God-centered worldviews, our actions and inclinations will align as such; if not, our efforts will definitively confirm otherwise. Again, Dr. Ravi Zacharias confirms, "belief is always part of worldview, but it is not always scrutinized to reason and rationality." He goes further, "Worldview must answer individual questions in correspondence to reality, and the sum of all answers must be coherent. "[20] Essentially, Dr. Zacharias confirms that belief is always a part of a worldview, but the truth, rationality and coherence may not be; anyone can be betrayed and undermined by their personal worldview. At this time in our history, it seems irrationality and incoherence have become the norm.

Social science confirms personal worldview and the strongholds of entrenched mindsets can be powerful motivators and justification for participating in causes. Today, when individuals can rapidly be transitioned into a "cause," then into "coalitions" (within the cause), and then form

---

[20] *Ravi Zacherias, the Logic Of God, Zondervan, 2019, pg 64*

coalitions into massive "revolutionary forces" (whereby everyone in the cause marches in lock-step toward a unified goal), serious social change can result. The time it takes for an individual's worldview and mindset to wholly transition into the mindset of a "radical revolutionary" has been truncated (mostly due to myriad factors including Social Media and mass communications). Today, massive social change can be achieved in months, not years. When Obama declared he "evolved" on the issue of homosexual marriage, almost overnight, it was accepted as a cultural norm, and all dissenters were immediately labeled "bigots" and "homophobes" and summarily dismissed. Again, Obama was a disciple of Saul Alinsky and self- described "revolutionary."

Importantly, when observing the spectrum of worldviews that now intersect and overlay culture and society, rationality and coherency are not terms that should come to mind. That's because "revolutionaries" are powered by pure, raw (most often) and unfiltered emotion. Strict reliance on ever-changing and unreliable human "emotion" to drive mass movements can oft times produce actions that belie truth, rationality and coherency. In the end, today, we observe singularity of focus, mission and objectives are being achieved through alliances of "strange bedfellows" with hugely disparate and conflicting principles.

It is easy to confirm that worldviews can be precipitated by mass social movements, and today are primarily driven by emotions. As has been stated, when individuals heavily rely on emotions to motivate actions, there is less consideration for "reason" or coherence, and raw action is used create momentum unto itself; in these times, raw emotions alone are somehow almost perfectly uniting toward "singularity" via mass revolutionary social movements; instead of mission chaos however, these social movements are in "lock-step" unity. How can this be? Sumantra Maitra *(senior contributor to The Federalist) poignantly observes,* "The modern left is a combination of two of the worst impulses in human history. First are the ultra-privileged bourgeoisie, which, having lost their old Judeo-Christian faith, are instinctively attracted to pre-civilized rituals, from overt sexuality to fewer familial ties. Consider Late Roman public orgies, and you get an idea. At the same time, human minds feel a gaping void that still needs to be filled by an alternate faith. It is in that intersection where this occultist, apocalyptic climate paganism comes from. It gives some privileged people a noble purpose."[21] He nicely summarizes the connection between Leftism and the intersectionality of an "alternate faith" (like "global warming"/"climate" in this instance) fills the void and provides a sense of noble purpose! This is exactly how our foe uses social movements to deceive and destroy us.

Our principal foe has been able to use his cunning and seduction to motivate people of dissenting backgrounds and conflicting worldviews, to reject their purpose and embrace the larger utopian goals that revolve around larger group identity....Leftism/Marxism/Statism! Again, if "New World Order"/globalism is accomplished, satan will be able to focus his influence on just a few people (central planning bureaucrats/masterminds) and in doing so produce world domination and utter devastation of the cosmic battlefield! The utopian objectives of Leftism (for example) blinds and binds; it blinds people to any number of personal differences in relation to morals and values they may have, while binding them to gleefully strive toward the same objective (most notably, authoritarian controls and social order dictated by "masterminds"). When this happens, we are not observing the emergence of conscientious social movements, we are witnessing a contrived "social revolution" underpinned by group-think. The ebb and flow of social revolutions are fundamentally dictated by massive numbers of people seeing the world through the same (collective) lens; as with almost all revolutions in history, brandishing a pervasive lens that focuses in on aggressive emotions like hatred and rage, binds people together and controls the fervency of revolutions. Today, social revolutions are being constituted based upon the most elusive utopian tenant of all, "equality."

"Equality," in the sense of everyone achieving exacting equal outcomes, is a fallacy. God has uniquely made each person and has given each a unique set of skills, talents and abilities to fulfill unique work(s). Because they hate the notion of God, however, utopian statists lie and contrive schemes for grievance and need for social revolution based on mythical notions of equality. C.S. Lewis, theologian, writer and one of the

---

[21] *Climate Worship Nothing More Than Rebranded Paganism, The Federalist Sept 26 2019, Sumantra Maitra*

preeminent intellectuals of all time, says this of equality, "The demand for equality has two sources — one of them is among the noblest, the other is the basest of human emotions. The noble source is the desire for fair play. But the other source is the hatred of superiority. At the present moment, it would be very unrealistic to overlook the importance of the latter. There is in all men a tendency (only corrigible by good training from without and persistent moral effort from within) to resent the existence of what is stronger, subtler or better than themselves. In uncorrected and brutal men, this hardens into an implacable and disinterested hatred for every kind of excellence. The vocabulary of a period tells tales. There is reason to be alarmed at the immense vogue today of such words as 'highbrow,' 'upstage,' 'old school tie,' 'academic,' 'smug,' and 'complacent.' These words, as used today, are sores — one feels the poison throbbing in them....There are two reasons for not attempting to [propitiate evil passions — to appease envy]. In the first place, you will not succeed. Envy is insatiable. The more you concede to it the more it will demand. No attitude of humility which you can possibly adopt will propitiate a man with an inferiority complex. In the second place, you are trying to introduce equality, where equality is fatal. Equality (outside mathematics) is a purely social conception. It applies to man as a political and economic animal. It has no place in the world of the mind. Beauty is not democratic — she reveals herself more to the few than to the many, more to the persistent and disciplined seekers than to the careless. Virtue is not democratic — she is achieved by those who pursue her more hotly than most men. Truth is not democratic — she demands special talents and special industry in those to whom she gives her favors. Political democracy is doomed if it tries to extend its demand for equality into these higher spheres. Ethical, intellectual, or aesthetic democracy is death."[22]

On paper, the myriad social movements connote significant differences. Differing goals and objectives and perceived "ideal outcomes" should preclude simpatico unification. But, if different movements are conditioned to see the world through the same "lens" (i.e. grievance, oppression, victimization, hate and/or "race") they can be blinded by reality and motivated by the objectives of the collective as the ultimate goal. With a collective

---

[22] C.S. Lewis: 'The demand for equality has two sources, the desire for fair play and hatred for superiority'. Caldron Pool 11/29/19

"lens" coloring and shading the world as systemically disproportional and oppressive, grievances due to lack of equality creates necessary inertia that coalesces disparate factions into a wholly united singular focus... revolution! Strategically speaking, this is a huge win for our foe because his side of the battle relies on a blind radical "revolution." He wins when people are blinded to personal stances (governed by morals, values and common sense), and therefore willingly act emotionally and duplicitously; active undermining an individual's personal stance or objective in dereferencing to the collective is a major underpinning of "revolution."

There is little doubt we have entered a revolutionary time in history. Our foe looks to consistently use untamed emotions as an integral part of social movements. With raw emotions as a driving force that fuels and propels cultural change through social movements, our foe can easily decimate the cosmic battlefield. Historically speaking, during periods of revolution, revolutionaries had little time to reflect, reason, or embrace rationality; there was only time to embrace emotion-driven action and act in order to decimate foe's. Strident "soldiers" of varying backgrounds, races, religions, and gender coming together to defeat a specified foe is what marks revolutionary wars. Strange bedfellows and uncommon (often contradictory) alliances are cobbled together with a common objective and it's the objective that binds the collective comrades while at the same time completely blinding to any personal differences! This is why we are now seeing so many movements of disparate contravening and contradictory motivations, aggressively unifying toward *social revolution*.

The social revolution is a cultural reality undergirded by the exact same mindset of contemporary war revolutionaries, with the only exception being social revolutionaries fight social wars and constructs, as opposed to wars requiring physical combat. Examples of social revolutionaries can be seen in modern-day Churches. There are many Churches that wholly embrace the lens of "race" (Social Justice, Black Liberation, CRT etc.) while asserting a true passion for God; in doing so, they show extreme deference to "race" (which actually undermines the Gospel of the Kingdom), with no regret or afterthought. They have no concept or foresight that because they dutifully intersect and coordinate with others fully embracing abortion/infanticide, they are actively participating in battle on satan's side of battleground against the very God they commit their lives to. This is just one example of how an entity or movement can perceive they're wholly principled and purposeful, but through collective zeal toward revolution can embrace delusional levels of duplicitous objectives that actually contradict their motives.

Many examples of relative incongruence precipitated by social revolutionaries abound these days. Since duplicitousness and incongruence tend to lead to doing the same thing over and over again yielding the same result, it is not an overstatement to confirm these times are marked by the literal definition insanity. Insanity is being aggressively pushed by social movements with the expectation participants conveniently overlook practicality and/or personal principle in deference to the collective good. When this occurs, intersectional alliances between factions on opposite ends of the spectrum become the norm, while logic and rationality are conveniently held in abeyance.

When President Trump was elected in 2016, many were quite surprised; "feminists" were outraged. Their anticipation of Hillary Clinton being the first female President was dashed, and they looked for "blood." Men, especially "White men in power," were immediately put on the defensive as they were targeted and labeled as purveyors of "toxic masculinity" and, therefore fundamental foe's of women. President Trump bore the brunt of their ire and was roundly castigated as a reprobate, "toxically masculine" misogynist. Decades-old purported Trump sound-bites, crass and bombast, and his image as a billionaire "playboy" gave new impetus to women, and women's rights marches were launched with renewed fury. Unfortunately, the women's march is a weaponized tool used to bludgeon and dispirit men, as opposed to being a movement that is bracing and positive toward all women. From the actual foe's perspective, this was a great opportunity to charge the cosmic battlefield with a new crop of "soldiers" on the front lines of the battle. He used the enemy he targets for total destruction, women, to embrace his tactics of hatred and rage in battle on his side in order to accelerate their own demise! Cunning and wickedly evil, indeed! Satan used this moment in history to blind women feminists from actually working on pragmatic and purposeful issues of justice for their constituents (women and girls) and with the tainted "lens" of hatred and rage, they now largely perceive the world through these negative emotions. With a pronounced focus on negative emotions of hatred and unfettered rage, little is accomplished as insanity accelerates the momentum of the revolution. There are many examples of illogical contravening contradictions precipitated via satan's intersectional revolutionary fruits; they are now being harvested via his war on women. Here are just a few examples:

Insane Intersections of the "Women's March"- After the election of President Donald Trump, women's groups and movements became incensed and quite motivated to coalesce around the rubric of "women's rights." With benign nomenclature of "women's rights" as its focus, the marches were well attended by women and men of every demographic. What was particularly troubling however, were demonstrations from "feminists" railing against "objectification of women," while at same time fully demonstrating contravening contradictions by proudly prancing around dressed as anatomically accurate vaginas and wearing vagina hats; any rational observer could easily see these women's vulgar and immodest "protests" only serve to precipitate their own ultimate "objectification!" Jewish women and other minority groups were also in attendance at these marches, but ironically, they were also cheering on and gleefully sharing intersectional collaborations with well-known anti-Semites; Jewish people cheering on and gleefully sharing the stage with anti–Semites? If those contravening intersectional collaborations are not mind- blowing enough, the Washington Times notes "women's march" leader(s) also advocate for Sharia law.[23] It should be noted that under Sharia law (a form of Islam) women are forbidden to drive cars, women are forced to wear head covering (and sometimes body covering), wives can be beaten by husbands, women's court testimony is unevenly weighed (in comparison to testimony from men), prepubescent girls can be forced into marriage, and a number of other acts that wholly relegate women to a lower status than men. Fundamentally, women participating in the Women's Marches stand side-by-side with these illogically disparate and conflicting anti-women mindsets! This is an example of how many willfully and dutifully subordinate personal passions for actual women's rights to pursue the overarching collective goal of social revolution.

---

[23]   *Washington Times Dec 24 2018 "Women's March leadership engulfed in racial and religious feuding."*

The only plausible explanation for how arcane, disparate ends of the spectrum can work together under the guise of protecting women (while in actuality harming women) is, they intersect as radical revolutionaries and commit to dutifully subvert individual passions of their respective movement (in this case, to stand for and protect women), in deference to the goal radical revolution. Based on Biblical realities of satan's war against women, these people have been cunningly seduced and blinded to fight against themselves and are regrettably aligned as soldiers on his side of the cosmic battlefield.

Intersectional madness of Gendercide & FGM- Gendercide is the systematic elimination of babies based on a specific gender. Contravening contradictions obviously goes unnoticed for women's rights advocates because even as baby girls are significantly and disproportionally harmed, women's rights advocates consistently encourage legislators to vote against any legislation that would prevent this horrid practice. It can be easily asserted that women rights begin in the womb! This statement should be the rallying cry for all women, and also an essential aspect of the women's rights movement, but instead it is conveniently overlooked and ignored. While women's rights advocates work diligently to deny significant numbers of baby girls the basic human right of birth, the Washington Examiner confirms they also work just as hard to "normalize" female genital mutilation (a tradition and practice of certain sects of Islam)![24] This would seem to be unfathomable, as it mutilates female genitalia (genital cutting/"female circumcision" procedure provided without medical reason or justification) in an attempt to control the behavior of girls and women. Feminist author, scholar and activist, Ayaan Hirsi Ali condemned feminists as follows, "feminists' failure to hold Muslims accountable for their misogyny: In Muslim communities, there is demand that women, girls, should be virgins and a woman's sexuality is to be controlled and this (FGM) is an effective and brutal way of doing that."[25] Female Genital Mutilation (FGM) is targeted at young girls, is very painful, and used to deter and prevent sexual intimacy and gratification. It's quite cynical

---

[24] *Washington Examiner Aug 03 2017. "Feminism Failure: Why don't feminists speak out against female genital mutilation?"*

[25] *Slate, Jalal Baig, May 01, 2017 "Female Genital Mutilation Isn't a Muslim Issue. It's a Medical Issue."*

and ironic to realize women's rights advocates proudly wear genitals (as a costume) and shout immodestly about sexual liberations, while at the same time, they tacitly align with practices that actually mutilate girls/women's genitals, control their behavior and dutifully prevent any sexual gratification. How do modern-day "feminists" reconcile this level of insanity? Feminists are now complicit with a willing embrace of working and collaborating with factions that fundamentally disempower and undermine girls and women? The radical revolution is the strategic element satan cunningly uses to blind in order to transcend otherwise rational thought and logic. During times of revolution, "the ends always justify the means." People with revolutionary mindsets, always view collective ends as taking precedence over individual/personal objectives. Clearly, duplicitous arcane insanity is predictable with radical revolutionaries.

Inconvenient intersections: Feminists imprimatur of Sex Assaults and Sex trafficking- Radical revolutionaries not only wholly embrace "intersectionality" (summarily defined as, interconnected social characterizations that intersect and overlap) inclusive of their own sexual objectification, but they couple it with embrace of bigoted anti-Semitism, gendercide, FGM (and other aforementioned disparate modalities). Ironically, their relative incoherence and insanity seem boundless as they seem keen to overlook the needs of the poorest and weakest girls/women in deference to revolution. To be sure, you would think that feminist and women's rights organizations would sternly protest if they found systemic instances of girls and women being routinely abused, sexually assaulted and sex trafficked. That said, when officials confirm tens of thousands of young girls and women are routinely subjected to such assaults each year as they trek to U.S. from South America and other regions south of U.S. borders, instead of attempting to keep these girls and women out of harms way, feminists and women's organizations show no regard for the welfare of these poor women; instead of insisting borders are secured and all inducements ended so females won't continue to make a dangerous trek virtually assuring sex assaults and trafficking, feminists and women's groups insist U.S. borders remain open and porous. A recent NY Times article, "You Have to Pay With your Body: The Hidden Nightmare of Sexual Violence on the Border,"[26]

---

[26] *New York Times Mar 03, 2019. "You Have to Pay With your Body: The Hidden Nightmare of Sexual Violence on the Border" by Manny Fernandez*

confirms the common practice of assaults of girls and women, and the level of grotesque human rights atrocities these migrants face when making the trek to the U.S. Ironically, all women's rights organizations remain quiet and complicit with these atrocities. From a basic human dignity standpoint, the thought of subjecting girls/women to loss of innocence and heinous assaults because of our inducement of open borders is a horrible price to pay. Radical revolutionaries, however, don't see the trauma of these women. Instead, they see a need to import endless numbers of poor and marginalized girls and women because they represent potential future cohorts that will help garner more power and influence of their respective women's movements; having to endure a traumatically assaultive trek is cavalierly viewed as a "means to an end!" Our foe is delighted when notable contradictions are completely unnoticed due to zealous radical revolutionaries' desire for open borders. Zealous revolutionaries are blindly led by avowed feminists as they tacitly encourage and enable an ever-increasing flow of sex assaults and human trafficking of girls and women. While these people are horribly victimized and abused under the imprimatur of women/feminists, satan's side of the cosmic battle against women is strengthened. This ironic intersection (open borders coupled with "women's rights") also helps reduce the cosmic battlefield between God and satan because many of those who endure this level of unbridled maltreatment are killed or permanently maimed/scarred in the process. Some never fully recover from this persistent trauma.

Feminists' Intersectional madness regarding racism- Based on sheer numbers, no single strategy helps satan wage war against women better than reducing the cosmic battlefield via abortion. As discussed in earlier chapters, our foe has waged an active and perpetual war against the woman and her offspring since the beginning of time. Over time, he's used evil despots to kill hundreds of millions of innocents in wars and famine, but abortion has been the single most effective tactic for reducing the battlefield; worldwide abortions are estimated at 1.5-2 billion innocent souls murdered! One of the most ironic intersections satan has used to masterfully blind feminists is, the intersection between Margret Sangers' disgusting racist schemes, and her use of Planned Parenthood to fully carry out her diabolical plans. On the one hand, Sanger is a well-known abhorrently evil racist committed to eliminating or significantly reducing Black and Brown populations, but on the other hand, she is a feminist hero and Founder of Planned Parenthood. Through cunning and seduction, our foe blinds feminists to the well- documented facts about Sanger and Planned Parenthood's schemes to actively eliminate Blacks and Hispanics that are being carried out to this very day, while at the same time ginning up emotions of feminists to actually audaciously complain about systemic racism! If not for now understanding satan's tactics on the cosmic battlefield, and having an understanding revolutionary social movements and entrenched mindsets, Planned Parenthoods audacious complaints about systemic racism would be unfathomably insane; fact is, they are unquestionably the single largest purveyor of racist hate and the largest contributor to satan's schemes to eviscerate women and their offspring!

Supreme Court Justice Ruth Bader Ginsberg, plainly states that she always thought Roe v. Wade was not about "women's rights," rather it was designed to "limit populations that we don't want to have too many of."

Some would attempt to deny claims of Planned Parenthoods racism, and their literal fight on satan's battlefield and against women, but any attempts to do so would be folly. The fact is, Margaret Sanger confirmed her racial hatred of Blacks while speaking at the Women's KKK rallies, calling Black's "reckless breeders" and "weeds that need to be eliminated," and notoriously proclaiming, "We don't want the word to go out that we want to eliminate the Negro population!"[27] Sanger was indeed satan's perfect tool! To be sure, Sanger's notorious hateful legacy continues to be carried forth to this very day via Planned Parenthood. Planned Parenthood still disproportionally targets Black and Brown populations by gratuitously placing clinics primarily in urban areas. Considering Blacks only make up about 13% of population and women making up half that (approx. 6.5%), then discounting by half of that to account for child bearing ages of 15-44 (approx. 3%), it's notable that Planned Parenthood has conveniently situated an overwhelming percentage of their "abortuaries" (60- 80% by some estimates[28]) in an attempt to cater to a demographic of only approx. 3% of their female

---

[27] *Article from Tradition, Family, Property , Nov 20, 2017*
[28] *The Federalist, "Yes, Plan ned Parenthood Targets And Hurts Poor Black Women", Willis L. Krumholz*

market! Sangers schemes to "eliminate Blacks" via Planned Parenthood targeting of Black communities have resulted in the Black baby deaths making up approx. 40% of all abortions while representing only 3% of the women demographics; disproportional gratuitous Black genocide has resulted. The only logical conclusion for Planned Parenthood's "success" in eliminating Blacks is, they continue to carry out Margret Sangers demonically inspired aspirations in accordance with her legacy and satan's dictates. Surely, those who work at Planned Parenthood and abortion center affiliations will attempt to deflect from diabolical and quite contrived historical schemes to eliminate Blacks. But, it should also be noted that Progressive "women's right champion," Supreme Court Justice Ruth Bader Ginsberg, plainly states that she always thought Roe v. Wade was not about "women's rights," rather it was designed to "limit populations that we don't want to have too many of."[29]

If you were to inquire of any feminist women organizations, they would confidently assure they wouldn't do anything racist or hurtful to Blacks and Hispanics, conversely, they would assure they are the most committed social movement for "justice" and racial equality. How is it that women/feminists can be so blind as to easily overlook Margret Sanger and Planned Parenthoods' foundation and pattern of racism? It's wholly illogical until you consider the fact that they are driven by the emotions of social revolution, not by rationality or principles of common sense. A great (but duplicitously cynical) example of Planned Parenthood's schemes is confirmed by their partnership with Black Lives Matter (BLM). To satan's glee, while women/feminists strongly assert Black lives actually do matter and march to portend such, they are aggressively carrying out a strategy of genocide specifically targeted at Black communities. Interestingly and hypocritically, BLM leaders strongly decry racism while at the same time stridently standing with Planned Parenthood, one the most racist modern-day organizations hell-bent (literally) on staying true to Margret Sanger's strategy of "eliminating Blacks." With all the public information about Sanger and Planned Parenthood, these strange bedfellows are clearly held together by conveniently blinding themselves to overlook historical truth

---

[29] CNS News, July 9, 2008, Chistopher Neefus- "Justice Ginsberg Says She Originally thought Roe v. Wade Was Designed To Limit Populations That We Don't Want To Have Too Many Of"

and facts in order to embrace a greater cause toward social revolution wholly. The intersection of racism and abortion has driven contravening contradictions to a fever pitch. This is just another glaring example of how satan uses women to battle on his side in an effort to utterly destroy and undermine women and offspring.

Intersectional incompatibility of Feminists and "Transgenders"-
Journalist Brandon Morse recently wrote an article questing, "Where Are The Feminists?" His article pointed out, "Feminists seem to be absent wherever women are suffering the most. Case in point, transgender activists and their allies are busy allowing boys and men to identify as female to gain access to women's locker rooms. This is particularly awful when you look at the fact that a lot of the locker rooms they're granting these boys access to are in public schools. Just earlier today, I wrote on a story about a school district in Illinois that ruled that a boy could access a girl's locker room if that's the sex he identifies as. Essentially, all a boy would have to do is say he feels like he's female that day, and there would be nothing teachers, parents, or fellow students could do to stop him from walking in there."[30]

One of the most astoundingly cynical ways our foe uses women to fight for him while destroying themselves is with the "Trans" movement. Feminists purposely deny the science of when life begins, and also deny confirmed science of biological genders. It is easy to assert, women/feminists are consummate "science deniers!" Notably, these denials target and hurt women in the exact ways our cunning adversary designed them; they help eliminate opposition on the cosmic battlefield. Gender dysphoria is the latest tactic our foe uses to normalize confusion. He knows that with a fog of confusion surrounding when life begins (scientists confirm at conception) coupled with confusion about God creating just two biological genders, he can skew human behaviors to go against (and affirmatively undermine) God and His divine creation. God's heart flows with love and compassion for all His creation, so we can only imagine His agony and disappointment when He sees His creation fighting on the opposite side of the cosmic battlefield and directly posing an affront to His

---

[30] *"Where are the Feminists?", Brandon Morse. Red State 11/2/2019*

divine order. When His creation doesn't rationally weigh and consider His Word (Bible), and instead allows itself to be conveniently used by satan to accelerate the attack on women, God is especially aggrieved.

Noted author, Raymond Victor Raehn offers keen observation as follows, "....the Critical Theorists of the Frankfurt School recognized that traditional beliefs and the existing social structure would have to be destroyed and then replaced. The patriarchal social structure would be replaced with matriarchy; the belief that men and women are different and properly have different roles would be replaced with androgyny; and the belief that heterosexuality is normal would be replaced with the belief that homosexuality is equally 'normal.'"[31] This appropriately encapsulates the history and background behind how we've arrived to the "Trans" movement.

The Trans movement is possibly one of the best examples of how motivated and desperate humanity is to embrace folly in pursuit of social revolution; in its desperation, it puts logic, wisdom and scientific/biological facts aside, and women and offspring are devastated in the process. God made biological men with a completely different DNA structure as compared to women. He ascribed appropriate DNA for roles and tasks He in His infinite, omniscient wisdom knew would be needed (based on His foresight and anticipation for His creation). The Transgender movement rejects DNA for male and female genders and instead postulates that genders are purely a social construct and can change and mutate to over 100 differing genders at any time (based on solely on the whims of the individual). Rejection of scientific/biological facts in order to embrace constructs not wedded to science or biological reality is pure insanity!

Intersectional insanity is definitively confirmed when feminist organizations cheer and gleefully stand on the side of people suffering from gender dysphoria as they compete against biological women in athletic events. Instead of assuring that girls and women are provided equal opportunity to fairly compete in athletic events in order to receive awards, prizes and scholarships that will help bolster confidence and allow them to

---

[31]   *The Historical Roots of Political Correctness, Raymond v. Raehn Published 9/3/2015*

succeed, women's organizations and groups are siding with "transgender women" (biological men) as they now are competing (and winning) in events that were strictly limited to competition between biological women. Scientific history confirms that in order for athletes (at any levels) to be given opportunities for fair and equitable competition, girls and women need to compete amongst themselves; God's biological reality makes it essential that there are separate events and categories clearly demarcated between men's and women's sports/competitions. In general, males are stronger, faster (with more lung capacity), and much bigger (with greater bone density) than females. This is not only problematic when considering how men outperform in sports, but we now also see feminists in full embrace of allowing biological men to share in the same private spaces likes showers, bathrooms, and other areas where females traditionally sought privacy and protection from men. What happened to the feminists/women who swore a commitment to fervently protect all women, support all women and affirm all women? Instead, we see them playing into satan's tactic of confusion. Confusion in this arena puts girls and women at risk of being abused and assaulted due to the intersectional insanity of enshrining Trans as preeminent protected demographic over and above the needs of biological women. Alas, feminist derelictions abound.

It is clearly manifest women/feminist groups are battling on their foe's side of the battlefield, and seem committed to fighting against themselves in helping him win the war. Instead of protecting women's rights, feminists now give the imprimatur of competitive largesse to the Trans community; clearly, girls and women are conveniently abused and undermined by intersectional feminists embracing collectivist machinations of social revolutions (as opposed to focus on justice for women). This demoralizes. Through tactics of demoralization, our mortal foe is able to scatter the battlefield as generations of biological females will now be raised with greater insecurities and confusion about their own identities. Ultimately, our foe would get a huge benefit as suicides significantly increase when insecurities and societal confusion run rampant. To be sure, NBC News confirms at least "half transgender males have attempted suicide."[32] Transgender suicide is off the charts compared

---

[32] *NBC News Sept 13, 2018 Half of transgender male teens have attempted suicide, study finds*

to other non trans demographics. The reason is clear, our eternal foe needs to limit the landscape and intensity of the cosmic battlefield against God and humanity. By self-elimination, satan gets humanity to embrace his battle as it eliminates and/or limits the effectiveness of God's creation. Humanity self-eliminates via abortion and via suicide, so these are the primary arenas where satan focuses feminist/women to do his bidding.

Through the arcane anathema of intersectionality, feminist groups and organizations who are otherwise committed to helping and supporting women, willingly blind themselves to logic and rationality in order to embrace a call to social revolution; the perfect case in point is confirmed by obvious hypocrisy and juxtaposition of how they protested and rallied against Justice Brett Kavanaugh's nomination to the Supreme Court (with no corroborating times, places or witnesses of purported sex/assaults), vs. how they rally for and fervently support Joe Biden even as he's accused of groping and sexual assault (with an abundance of significant witnesses, including time/dates and correlating evidence).[33] Somehow, the "believe all women" mantra that overwhelmed women's marches and protests during Kavanaugh hearings has conveniently disappeared without even the slightest hint of shame for grotesque hypocrisy.

With the feminist movement becoming more tolerant of arcane duplicitousness and lack of consistency and coherence associated with supporting women, what are we to conclude? President James Monroe once stated, "When the people become ignorant & corrupt...they become the willing instruments of their own ruin." That said, an obvious conclusion we can discern is, the feminist movement has seemingly become a willing instrument of its own ruin. Revolutionary zeal of feminist movements has allowed them to become mostly irrelevant and undermined (including Women's Lib, #MeToo, #BelieveAllWomen, and etc.). They have given primacy to political and cultural activism, and therefore transitioned away from the mission to help and protect women around the world (even as women continue to experience indignities associated with being maligned and persecuted). Today's feminist movement is committed to wielding its collective powers (granted

---

[33] *National Review, April 27, 2020 "The hypocrisy on Tara Reade is a National disgrace," The Editors*

by respective followers) as a tool for political and social activism; most notably, this has lead to a revolution of Leftist Progressivism. "Revolutionaries" precipitating the current social/cultural revolution are leading society in one direction. That one direction is toward statism; again, statism empowers masterminds within governments to control societal behaviors via mandate (Socialism/Marxism/Communism are our foe's desired statist forms of government, as they are tyrannical at best and ultimately totalitarian). As statism is adopted, our foe gains the ability to cunningly devour humanity with just a few masterminds, allowing significant control and trajectory of the cosmic battlefield. Through the need for expediency and control, our foe covets the idea of being able to immediately transform cultures and societies through a heavy-handed totalitarian government apparatus, and statism (leading to "One World Government") provides it. He believes strategies and tactics using the lens of hatred and rage, revolutionary social movements, entrenched mindsets, contravening contradictions, diabolical intersectionality, and all other forms of machinations that blind humanity to his schemes, will assure success in his war against God and humanity. The fact is, just like the delusions he has been able to get so many to embrace, he's also horribly deluded! The fact is, God has already won the war for women (and her offspring), and satan is merely biding his time.

As we can see, satan has used his war to intersect and overlay almost every cross-section in culture! It pinpoints then feeds off every grievance while underlining every deviancy. It's interesting to note that satan has blinded to the extent there are myriad disparate factions wholly unified via a "cottage industry" of grievances; in essence, all fomentations of these movements including race, gender, political parties, grievance and etc., are emotional triggers used to coalesce and unite. More pointedly, they are actually mere "distractions" our foe uses as fodder to drive emotions and divide while forcing culture & society in one direction...toward his fundamental utopian instruments of Leftism/Progressivism.

The root of the tree has been cut and the "fruit" of the war on women has been unveiled. Now it's time to turn the tide of the war and begin waging it against our committed foe in order to gain the upper hand in

...all fomentations of these movements including race, gender, political parties, grievance and etc., are emotional triggers used to coalesce and unite. More pointedly, they are actually mere "distractions" our foe uses as fodder to drive emotions and divide while forcing culture & society in one direction...toward his fundamental utopian instruments of Leftism/Progressivism

the war on women. With God's wisdom, grace and mercies, we can storm the battlefield on behalf of God and humanity and forever turn away from the cunning serpent satan.

Based on all aforementioned evidence confirming peculiar and quite illogical intersectional alliances, it is easy to confirm there are contravening contradictions that do not at all comport with Dr. Zacharias' description of the need for worldview coherency. It is profoundly obvious there is a complete lack of coherency between any of the aforementioned contravening factions. To be sure when we wind it all back, we can see how intersectional contradictions are rooted in dysfunctional cultural movements, and how dysfunctional cultural movements are rooted in social revolutionary mindsets, and how current social revolutionary mindsets are rooted in utopian driven Leftism/Progressivism, and how Leftism/Progressivism is fundamentally rooted in statism, and how statism is rooted in our foe's strategy for "one world" powers, and how our foe's "one world" government powers schemes are rooted in the need for population control, and how population controls are our foe's ways to control the cosmic battlefield, and how control of the battlefield against God and humanity are rooted in satan's delusions of winning the war in this realm, and how the war in this realm is rooted in the war that God declared started in the Garden of Eden, and how the war in Garden of Eden is rooted in the targeting of women and offspring, and how women and offspring became targets due to transfer of power and authority from Adam and Eve, and how Adam and Eve are the first fruits and first roots that begat God's power and authority to rule and reign in this realm. This is how we reconcile what's happening today! This is how we observe the schemes, tactics and strategies of our mortal foe. This is the beginning of how we change the trajectory of the battlefield; ultimately, we arrive at the woman and baby! This is the crux of the cosmic battle being waged in this realm, so we must redouble commitment to battle and fight for women and offspring.

The truth about the "fruit" of satan's war is wholly inconvenient for many. Due to our foe's stronghold on the minds of many, there will be many attempts to disprove what has been presented and grounded as objective fact, with a response of abject "hate." Our foe is exposed, so this is to be expected. Legendary novelist and journalist George Orwell once stated, "The further society drifts from the truth the more it will *hate* those who speak it." Since our foe's modus operandi is grounded in hate, surely his followers and "soldiers" will hate accordingly....

Closing Argument

The biggest intersectional contravening contradiction is women fighting against themselves! This is what it looks like when women declare war on themselves. When involved in a war (and especially "revolution"), you lose self-awareness, and capacity for self- reflection. As such, women have become quick to shed innocent blood, their own blood and the blood of their offspring. In this, they are following satan, loving what he loves and wanting what he wants. The fact is, women cannot dislodge from this notably illogical chaos unless and until they switch battlefields. We all need God. We cannot begin to look like and reflect Christ while fervently fighting on the battlefield against Him! Wonder why the body of Christ is so fractured and dis-united? A significant factor is, too many who profess "Faith" (generally) are literally fighting on the opposite side of the battlefield wholly opposite and against God! It's time for us to awaken and fight on God's side. We should now begin to discern since we desperately want to fight and win in the battle for women, the fundamental solutions for fighting and winning this battle are Spiritual ones!

PART III
TURNING THE TIDE

Defeating The Foe By Winning For Women
And Offspring

CHAPTER 11

WHAT YOU "LOOKIN FOE?"

Opening Statement

If we agree with what's been unveiled about our cosmic battle and war thus far, we would conclude there's a war that rages against all humanity via women (and offspring). We would conclude it started at the beginning of humankind and it is led by our principal foe. We must then conclude it is wholly impossible to be committed to our Faith, while now knowingly standing with/on the side of our foe. This presents a paradox! Some would like to continue doing what they've been doing and supporting what they've been supporting, but the foe has now been revealed and as God's eternal enemy. Any enemy of God, by definition, is an enemy of His children! To remain vigilant about our foe, we must be able to identify him and his diabolical schemes destined to destroy humanity.

The only way to assure we're fighting on God's side of the cosmic battlefield and using our energies and resources to battle against our hateful foe, to affirmatively identify and confirm satan and all of his schemes. Keen awareness of relentless hateful plots and subtle schemes designed to undermine will help mitigate being duped into soldiering on our foe's side of the battlefield; it will also protect, restore, and heal the soul. It is necessary to maintain purposeful vigilance in the development of a sharpened sensitivity to perceive our hateful foe.

It has now been unveiled that there is a definitive war on women. It has been further revealed that this is a cosmic war initiated at the beginning of humanity and will continue throughout eternity. Our eternal foe hates us; this foe hates us all and intends to utterly destroy humanity as a way to spite and triumph over the God of all creation. His tactics and strategies have culminated in many of the righteous (righteous people of Faith, and those with good and just intentions) being deceived and unwittingly standing and fighting on his (foe's) side of the battlefield. All socio/cultural chaos can be attributed to the demonic realm. Satan's modus operandi is to "seek all whom he may devour"; he seeks to destroy and devour humanity through chaotic social movements and "radical revolutionaries" as they significantly impact culture and societies. While our foe would like his war and tactics to remain shrouded and concealed due to his vile brazen hatred directed at women and offspring, we now have the capacity to observe and discern his diabolical antics; the sheer level of extreme violence and maltreatment toward women and offspring confirms it. The question we must ask ourselves is, "Are we ready to confront our entrenched mindsets to confront our mortal foe, so we can begin turning the tide of war in favor of God's side of the battle?" As opposed to normal, clichéd "Of course I'm on God's side," this question impales at a depth of the soul, and needs serious consideration; flippant retorts that connote cavalier consideration, can't be taken seriously. Only a truly righteous response will suffice. But what is a "righteous response?"

"Righteousness exalts a nation, but sin is a reproach to any people"~ Proverbs 14:34. This verse was central to the great Civil Rights pioneer, the honorable Frederick Douglass. Just as we perceive in these times, Douglass perceived there was a dearth of righteous people during his era. Douglass is known for this profound declaration, "I have one great political idea ... That idea is an old one. It is widely and generally assented to; nevertheless, it is very generally trampled upon and disregarded. The best expression of it, I have found in the Bible. It is in substance, "Righteousness exalted a nation; sin is a reproach to any people. This constitutes my politics – the negative and positive of my politics, and the whole of my politics ... I feel it my duty to do all in my power to infuse this idea into the public mind, that it may speedily be recognized and practiced upon by our people."[34] In a word, "righteousness" is the goal! It is not that there weren't righteous people then, or even now. The issue we've always faced is our foe can easily manipulate even righteous minded people, and he deceives them into seeing the world via race, hatred, animus, oppressions, grievance and etc.. When this happens, people feel justified while acting untoward toward others (without second thought), and use inertia of their actions to defend their contrived mindsets. If the lens through which we perceive the world is very narrow in scope, we will have a limited view of righteous alternatives, and this blinds us from realizing we are fighting a cosmic battle against a foe not limited to this realm. To begin taking righteous actions, we must begin to see the world through a worldview lens that consistently conveys the cosmic reality of a binary battle with our foe; surely the "fog of war" skews our view, but we must grow sensitive to his schemes as he relentlessly wages war against women and offspring. This is the dividing line between being able to discern righteousness vs. unrighteousness and good vs. evil!

Ephesians 6:12 confirms, "We wrestle not against flesh and blood, but against principalities, against powers, against the rulers of darkness of this world, against spiritual wickedness in high places." Whew! If this is how the battle is being waged against us, "How in the world do we identify our foe and his accouterments destined to destroy humanity (mostly via women and offspring) going forward?" Righteousness comes from being able to discern. Discernment going forward involves just being able to confirm which side of the battlefield you're on, and which side others around you are on. Those on your side of the battlefield will lock arms with you, and battle and fight to forestall satan's onslaught against women and offspring. In this regard, new understanding of the cosmic battlefield and our foe's war on women and offspring simplifies our relationships and commitments. Here forward, our relationships and support are not about which Political Party someone belongs to, our personal traditions, our race, gender, religious denominations, academic research, nobility, or any other distinction. It's simply about discernment about which side of the battlefield you (and/

---

[34]   *Frederick Douglass, "The Frederick Douglass Papers," John Blassingame, editor (New Haven: Yale University Press, 1982), Vol. 2, p. 397, from a speech delivered at Ithaca, New York, October 14th, 1852*

or others) are fighting on. If one asserts they're fighting on God's side of the battle in support of women and offspring, their actions confirm it via a dogged commitment that comports with not taking any actions that hurt or undermine them. This also means they'll wholly reject all officers (politicians and leaders) and organizations (social movements and revolutionaries) who assert avowed support to harm them (via abortion/infanticide).

Have we now entered an era when we have to hold one another accountable to a "litmus test?" No. There's no litmus test, rather we're being compelled to conduct a "battleground test." God's battleground test is a simple assessment as to whether one is standing and fighting on His side or on the serpent's/satan's side?" Sincere soul searching and introspection confirms which side you stand and battle. If you are in full support of abortion/infanticide, which side of the battlefield are you stridently fighting on? If you engage in prostitution, which side are you on? If you have a penchant toward domestic violence, which side are you on? If you support radical women's marches and organizations (like racist/bigoted Planned Parenthood), which side of the battle are you on? If you support Political Parties that encourage and desire to spread abortions around the world, which side are you on? If you support political candidates who are stridently pro-abortion, which side of the battlefield are you on? Certainly, there are too many instances and examples to consider. Still, the point is, if you are involved in supporting or performing any act that maligns, undermine, and disempowers women and offspring (babies), you are actively fighting on satan's battlefield! There's no way to sugarcoat this observation; Biblical fact compels it!

> *Have we now entered an era when we have to hold one another accountable to a "litmus test?" No. There's no litmus test, rather we're being compelled to conduct a "battleground test."*

Our foe's biggest advantage in his war on women is his ability to conceal devious schemes that encourage humanity to gleefully "soldier on" and battle on his side of the battlefield. He knows if humanity ever becomes adept at observing demonic tactics and strategies, the trajectory will turn and the cultural battleground will tilt in favor of the righteous. Going forward, adeptly identifying our foe is the way "the righteous" will weaken him. We should now be able to identify and reject satan's demonic schemes when he uses emotionally charged rants about "racism" as a way to get people to battle on his side of the battlefield. When he uses "White Supremacy," "toxic masculinity," "women's reproductive health (abortion)," skin color, political ideologies and affiliations, and any number of other socio/cultural distinctions, we should now be able to discern these as demonic distractions. Again, our foe uses these mere shadows to emotionally charge humanity into a blind rage so as to justify fighting on his side of the battle while concealing the reality of his war against God and humanity.

Wisdom and discernment are effective tools we can use to blunt the onslaught of emotional distractions precipitated by the demonic realm. Wisdom and discernment about satan's battle against women and offspring will motivate us to reject his labels and generalizations while confidently supporting people who may have been obliquely deemed "White Supremacists," "White Christian Evangelicals," "racist", "homophobic," xenophobic," "sexist," Conservative, Republican, misogynist, "privileged" and any number of other negative connotations, as long as they are confirmed to be battling on God's side of the battle line. These characterizations are gross generalizations spoken in tones of certitude in an attempt to get society to genuflect to demonic schemes. We have to remember, satan is "the accuser of the brethren " (Rev 12:10), and since he pioneered name-calling, he will relentlessly use this tactic to harangue and harass in hopes of bludgeoning humanity (especially those who dissent against political correctness) into submission. Those on his side of the battlefield are "soldiers" using these very tactics to accomplish the goals of our foe. Wisdom and discernment give the capacity to observe how our foe uses generalized characterizations to malign and disparage as a way of encouraging blind conformity within his ranks. We now know, conformity to our foe's schemes mean we actually actively fight and war against God and His battle for humanity.

We can clearly identify our foe via his works! When commanded to strictly adhere to politically correct speech, actions, and mindsets, we've identified the works of our foe. When we are pressured to act in accordance with the demand for conformity to prevailing cultural mindsets established by "elites" in media, arts, academia, and socio/political spheres, we've identified our diabolical foe at work! When we are castigated for utilizing our God-given capacity for "free-thinking," to the extent we reject prevailing parlance around "Social Justice," "Women's Right To Choose"/"Reproductive Rights," Critical Race Theory/"White Privilege," Black Liberation Theology, and utopian dreams of Marxism, we have confirmed our diabolical foe's works! Those who demean, demonize and castigate others for being "free-thinkers" (those who reject cultural "group-think" and political correctness) are definitively soldiers who battle on our foe's side of the battlefield. Let that sin in! How many individuals have we supported and encouraged that are on our foe's battlefield? How many organizations have we been involved with that dutifully progress our foe's agenda? How many of our foe's schemes have we been caught up in with sincere desire to support "women and children," but are now confirmed as tools designed to undermine and destroy them as part of satan's war on God and humanity?

Identification of our foe and his schemes simplifies our capacity to discern the motives and intentions of others we may be connected to. We no longer assess based on Political affiliation, skin color, "wealth"/status, or any other arcane generalization; the only criteria and assessment to be made going forward revolves around determining which side of the cosmic battlefield someone's on. Assessing battlefield provides soul-piercing, gut-wrenching reality-check that can help maneuver to a place of contrition, and then enable one to be "set free" (from all strongholds) in order to be powerfully used on God's side of the battle…

Closing Argument

Satan's works are now manifestly evident. His schemes designed to force all into socio/cultural conformity, to believe a certain way (and demean and castigate all dissenters), and to vote a certain way in order to enshrine and usher in authoritarian world governments, have now been fully unveiled. We are left with a revelation that confirms we have been fighting and battling in a cosmic war destined to undermine God and humanity via women and offspring. At the base of our souls, we are forced to confirm what side of the battlefield we will stand and fight on. If we support and endorse ONLY those individuals and institutions that uphold the value of women, summarily validated by the commitment to "life," we are on God's side. If we don't, we are on definitively on our foe's side of the battlefield! This is the simple yet critical issue, "Which side of the battlefield does your "fruit" confirm you're fighting on?"

CHAPTER 12

VICE-GRIPPING: FREED FROM CULTURAL VICE

Opening statement

Satan's battlefield is littered with landmines of cultural vice. Being firmly planted on his side of the battlefield allows one to be overtaken and defiled by vice, avarice, and any number of negative cultural strongholds. In an attempt to control observations and impulses that keep humanity tethered to his side, satan uses stronghold and vice. Perceiving strongholds and vice from the standpoint of recognizing that these are satan's purposed tools to wage war on women and offspring, will enable breaking away from his battlefield and being permanently set free! A critical step toward freedom is to be rid of vice...

All humanity is gripped and swept into a preexisting cosmic battle. Based on our actions and personal ideology/mindset, we wittingly or unwittingly chose which side of the battle we are fighting on. It is important to note that satan's side offers a losing proposition (it's designed to undermine God and all humanity via women and offspring) and by definition, is ultimately the losing side of the cosmic battlefield. If our foe is a cosmic loser, why does he seem to succeed with so much of humanity battling on his side? The fact is, this is battle is a real war, and all wars are "fluid" and experience cycles of success and failures (on either side of the battle) with ebbs and flows; because the battle between God and the serpent/satan is being waged in this realm, ebbs, and flows of the battle are conditioned based on the socio/cultural trajectory of humanity. With plenty of experience and knowledge of base frailties of humankind, our foe sets demonic traps and landmines in anticipation of gripping and enrapturing human minds with vice and myriad addictions. Vice and avarice are the most prominent attributes shared among throngs of soldiers on our foe's side of the battlefield. Fundamentally, he uses vice, addictions, and proclivities that captivate and ensnare the mind like a vice grip. With a vice grip-like hold, our foe virtually squeezes the confines of our soul until he encapsulates and conquers it into an almost unbreakable hold. Notably, snares, traps, and vice are the antitheses of what happens on God's side. God's side of the battle offers freedom from all vice and entanglements. He loves His creation and desires it to be set free! "Freedom" is a fundamental attribute soldiers share in common on God's side of the battlefield.

There is a stark contrast between opposing forces situated on each side of the battlefield. Besides the fact that one side is wholly committed to destroying women and offspring, and the other wholly committed to honoring and upholding them, on an interpersonal basis, one side provides nothing but strongholds and bondage (satan/demonic realm), while the other (God's realm) is purposed that all "soldiers" are to be set free from all such entanglements. The pivot from one side of the battle to the other requires the surrender of vice. In order to transition to God's side, all vice must simply be surrendered, and He will welcome you and help you fight on His side of the battle. Surrender of all vice is especially important because, when it comes to battling for women and offspring, most all vice and/or addictions are at least tangentially rooted in the battle between our foe and humanity.

There are many vices and addictions our foe uses in an attempt to ensnare humanity permanently. One of the most destructive is pornography. Pornography may seem like one of those "private," benign, and quite personal vices, but in actuality, it is the consummate tool out foe uses to change thought processes and perceptions in an all-out assault God's chosen vessel for birthing and nurturing humanity...women! Based on the satan's declared war against women and babies, we can easily observe the level of inhumane assaults he has hoisted onto both targets. With tens of millions of babies being wantonly slaughtered annually (in the most horrendous ways) and women/girls being unscrupulously preyed upon and dehumanized, we can easily see these acts as precipitated by the demonic realm. The satanic battlefield is littered with "landmines" that act as strongholds intended to ensnare the very soul of his soldiers. Due to the malevolent destruction and chaos it promulgates, pornography is preeminent among our foe's battlefield landmines.

> *With tens of millions of babies being wantonly slaughtered annually and women/girls being unscrupulously preyed upon and dehumanized, we can easily see these acts as precipitated by the demonic realm.*

It's destructive, degrading, dehumanizing, and yet quite pervasive! Pornography is our foe's' attempt to humiliate and decimate women and girls (mostly); it reduces God's glorious females to merely physical commodities and sexual objects. Again, our foe delights in undermining God's creation in such ways. Since pornography is mostly done in secret, many participate in it to the extent it becomes an addiction. As with any other addictions, pornography progressively grips and pummels the soul into submission to its insatiable demand for "more." With a seemingly never-ending cycle of "more," pornography grips mass numbers of people into more leering, more degradation, more voyeurism, just more appetite for "more!" Ultimately, people become desensitized to their regressive level of base inhumanity, and from there, the need for more can easily escalate into a "slippery slope" of taking actions like participating prostitution (as "buyer" or "seller"). From there, it can easily escalate further into participating in sex slavery, child slavery, and sex assault arenas. All these acts culminate in satan's grand scheme to gratuitously undermine and dehumanize women (and girls); again, God specifically chose and entrusted women as preeminent vessels to birth and nurture all of humanity. When you consider a foe who hates humanity and is at war against women, it easy to see how pornography is an addition borne of the demonic realm and wholly representative of his battlefield strategy! Pornography is satan's ultimate dehumanizing objectification of humanity, those destined to be God's "image-bearers."

In his book "Jezebel's War with America," Dr. Michael Brown says this of Pornography, "In the end porn makes women less womanly and men less manly since there is far more to being a woman and being a man than having sex. Porn even makes us less human, reducing us to animal status, living only to fulfill lusts. And to those with sensitive consciences, porn brings shame, self-hatred, depression, and more. The risk is surely not worth the reward, the pleasure not worth the penalty."[35] Since pornography is a horrible, dehumanizing addiction that ultimately drains the soul of morals and values (and any semblance of Godliness), how can humanity break from it? It may sound too simplistic, but recognizing there's a cosmic war, a foe, and the respective battlefield (strategies and tactics) is the key to getting rid of vice and receiving restoration of the soul. Consider this, if before engaging in pornography, you visualize the battlefield and observe how satan seeks to now use you as a tool to promulgate pornography as act in his war on women, you may begin to change behavior. If you consider that the foe who hates humanity is purposed to destroy it through individuals who participate or proliferate pornography, you may begin to change behavior. If you consider that or eternal foe seeks to continue the escalation of pornography so as to make it acceptable to children (via purposeful desensitizing tactics via schools), so they become enslaved/ sex trafficked, and further tilt his battlefield advantage, you may begin to change behavior. The fact is, every act surrounding pornography is used to enthrone further enshrine and empower satan, our chief foe, in the battle for women. We begin to change the battlefield trajectory by being set free from this diabolical vice.

Sex assaults and child/human trafficking are other vice and addictions use to degrade and undermine God and humanity. Sex assaults are part and parcel of the human trafficking epidemic; as abuse goes, you cannot have one without the other! Our foe also uses these landmines on his battlefield as addictions. Some people have been so maligned, confused, and wrecked with soul- sickness; they actually feel nothing as they participate in harming others (including little children). For them, the addiction revolves around ensuring personal gratification at all costs. The gratification can come from making money on trafficked individuals, or from using and abusing trafficked individuals for sexual pleasure. Either way, morals, values, ethics don't exist for people smitten with wanting to

---

[35] *"Jezebel's War with America," Michael L. Brown Ph.D., Frontline Charisma Media Copyright 2019*

enslave and/or rape those who have been sex trafficked. What's especially telling about our foe's tactics in this arena, is his addicting people to the "appetite" of raping of little children. Only a demonic foe with an agenda to destroy humanity can use such brazen horrors and darkness to undermine God and humanity.

Dr. Michael Brown says this of the scourge of human trafficking, "...This is horrific beyond words...It is estimated that worldwide roughly one million children are sold into sex slavery or forced labor every year, including forty thousand per year in America, which amounts to 109 children per day. ...This is so sickening, so disturbing, and so troubling that it is amazing that God has not vomited out the entire nation, that He has not sent down fire from heaven, that He has not wiped us out once and for all. Who can imagine such evil, let alone perpetuate it? Who can conceive of kidnapping little children-even toddlers and infants- then selling them into sex slavery, where they are forced into violent acts for adult viewers?" Intense soul-sickness pervades the hearts of many, and they are on the "front lines" of satan war against women and offspring. While they have worked heartily for their demented master (satan), they too can be set free. If one can begin to observe the reality that all acts of assault/sex assault/child rape/human trafficking as fundamentally enabling and empowering satan in his battle against God, perhaps some who have participated in such acts may pause their actions and get help. Here's the bottom line, any persons who precipitate acts (or actions) intended to inflict pain, suffering, and/or causing untoward maltreatment of women and children are confirmed to be literally working on behalf of our foe; it's an indisputable fact that person is literally battling on the serpent/satan's side of the battlefield. Does that also include those who participate in domestic violence? What about adulterers?

> *...the realization that any untoward maltreatment (assaults/abuse, prostitution, trafficking, adultery, abortion/infanticide, violence and etc.) directed toward God's precious vessels (women/girls and offspring) confirms the literal act of having taken up "arms" to solder on satan's side*

Out foe is keen to undermine women in as many ways as possible. He has sought to destroy women in as many ways as can possibly be humanly imagined. Even with his onslaught of purposeful undermining, women still thrive all over the world. They are not only God's chosen vessels for life and nurturing, but they possess interminable fortitude and inner strength that can carry them through as not only "survivors," but "more than overcomers." Satan seeks to use domestic violence to purposefully malign, which can then lead to immobilizing insecurities, and then lead to the ending of the life of women and girls; yet, even with our foe's most strident desires and strategies designed to destroy, women mostly thrive by far! He has also spurred sex addiction in adulterous spouses and uses their derelictions in the hope of permanently damaging the soul of women. What cannot be overlooked is, all these actions are targeted and focused on women as an assault against God and humanity; again, anyone participating in these acts is confirmed "soldiers" on satan's side of the battlefield. Countless multitudes (including Pastors and Clergy of all types) participate in these acts and will try to balk at this assertion. But if we simply look at Biblical facts and leave emotions and attempts at plausible justifications out of it, you can only arrive at one conclusion in this matter; there is no plausible deniability. Facts confirm, many have been deceived and are wittingly or unwittingly actively fighting against God and for our foe! The only way to change the trajectory is to change course. The way to change the course requires contrition and repentance.

Even with the highest levels of personal commitment to personal morals, values, ethics, and a commitment to "doing the right thing," it seems almost nothing has been able to stop (or even slightly stem) the onslaught of satanic degrading and inhumane assaults on women and girls. Since many of these affronts to our personal and collective conscience can be done in private, and are viewed as just personal, benign "little addictions," they have continued unabated. The power to overcoming these grotesque evils against women and girls comes from the realization that simplistic myopic view of being stricken with "little" personal sins or addictions does not provide enough disincentive; it's not about just trying to overcome "personal sins," it's about actually seeing/realizing which side you're standing and fighting on the battlefield as you partake in these sins and addictions. Coming to the realization that any untoward maltreatment (assaults/abuse, prostitution, trafficking, adultery, abortion/ infanticide, violence and etc.) directed toward God's precious vessels (women/girls and offspring) confirms the literal act of having taken up "arms" to solder on satan's side of the cosmic battlefield while allowing him to gratuitously use and control people in his war against God and humanity, provides quite another level of disincentive for those struggling in the arena of "personal sins." Observing our battlefield plight in these terms pierces the soul and provides an appropriate "gut-check" to those currently and potentially addicted to satanic landmines; no one wants to be literally fighting for satan against God knowingly.

Everyone arrives at a point when we must reconcile our position on the battlefield. Will you be a friend of God in His fight or a part of the horde from a determined foe that fights against God? Again, there is no "in-between," "safe space," or "neutral" position. We've confirmed many of the almost endless acts that can be committed as a foe against God, so there should be no doubt about where you chose to stand. That said, "Where do you stand?" Are you committed to God or the serpent/satan? As Dr. Ravi Zacharias states, is your personal stance (or worldview) coherently consistent with origin, meaning, morality, and destiny? Your new or renewed destiny begins now!

Closing arguments

Our foe has purposely and severely tilted the landscape of cultural vice against women/girls and offspring. His machinations designed to overwhelm females with malevolent chaos is not a normal progression of culture and societies; it's not cultural inertia! Satan has purposely shepherded a strategically dystopian mindset and stronghold about women/girls and offspring (in general) that allow many just to view this precious segment as mere "objects" to be gratuitously used, abused, and/or cast aside (killed) on a whim. People involved in any of these activities are actively warring on satan's side of the cosmic battlefield. This means their actions are not "personal" or "benign," it means they are stridently warring and battling against God on the cosmic battlefield. There is hope, however! The pivot comes from a broken and contrite heart asking for forgiveness...

CHAPTER 13

FORGIVENESS: STRATEGIC BATTLE WEAPON "FOR- GIVING"

Opening Statement

The sheer gravity related to what has been uncovered about our foe, his war on women, and our place on the cosmic battlefield, may have some feeling lost and hopeless. The reality of the matter is, virtually everyone on the planet has participated in some way (mostly unwittingly) committing atrocious acts that undermine women/girls (and babies) while fighting on satan's side against God. For many professed Christians (like myself), it is a sobering realization to now know that while they've committed their lives to God and sincerely strive to love and live for Him, they now have another area of base depravity in the recess of their own soul that has to be dealt with. The first step to winning this battle requires the purification of the soul, which starts with forgiveness. As with all other areas where we fall short, the way forward involves purposeful acts of repentance and forgiveness.

Everyone starts his or her Spiritual journey in a wretched condition. This is a fact of life for all humanity, and we cannot forget it! Finding additional areas of our soul that God (by His mercies) pinpoints as needing to be addressed, simply confirms there are more areas He (alone) needs to build and refine in us. His work in us is never complete. This is especially true with respect to the cosmic battlefield, as it is a never-ending eternal battle. God is quite determined to make each one a strident soldier on His side and reveals more and more of His plans as we commit to journey with Him. Ultimately, we (individually) have to take a stand in the firm declaration as to what side of the battle we are committed to fighting, and appropriately pivot (if need be) in order to reconcile our actions and intentions while bringing coherence to our stance. Our many (seemingly endless) derelictions may make the pivot from one side of the battlefield to the other seem ominous, but it simply requires solemn acts of forgiveness and repentance. On the surface, this may seem somewhat inconsequential, but it fundamentally becomes the battle within the deep crevices of the soul that dictates our actions in relation to the cosmic battle. If we are unresolved (as opposed to resolute), we may go through the motions of repentance and forgiveness, but unnecessarily struggle with accepting God's forgiveness of sins and memories of acts we have already been dutifully forgiven of. David is a man forever immortalized as "a man after God's own heart"(1 Sam 13:14). He is a great example of how to process the tension of God's desire to forgive and our ability to graciously accept His forgiveness without constantly revisiting and rememorizing and reliving deeds that even God chooses not to remember.

King David's story in the Bible is a good parallel because it confirms what can happen when we allow leering eyes, voyeurism/pornography, lust, and adultery to override our commitment to Biblical wisdom and prudence. In other words, it is a story we can all relate to. 2 Sam.11-12 summarily confirms David's story as follows: It was a time of war, but King David stayed home to relax and rejuvenate. After napping one afternoon, he looked out from his palace roof and noticed a beautiful woman bathing. He inquired about her, sent for her, and took her to his bed. Then he sent her home. David thought his liaison was fundamentally "benign and secret," but later receives a message from Bathsheba that she was pregnant. In an attempt to cover-up his adulterous folly, he schemes to have Bathsheba's husband home from the battlefront, where he was serving as one of David's soldiers. After commending Uriah for his good service, he dismisses him to return home to his wife, thinking that this would make Uriah think the baby was his own. But Uriah refused to go in with his wife because he felt it unfair for him to partake in such delights while with his fellow soldiers who were camping out on the battlefield. David then resorts to a scheme to have Uriah killed in battle. After receiving the devastating news her husband is dead, Bathsheba then agrees to become a wife of David. David again assumes he's covered all tracks, but God sends the prophet Nathan to confront David using an analogy of a famous story about the rich man and the poor man with only one ewe lamb. Ultimately, David recognizes his sinful ways and repents. God forgives David but not before a long list of terrible consequences. Again, this story is poignant and important because even as David participated in leering, pornography/lust, adultery, and killing, he is forever memorialized as "a man after God's own heart!" This means that while we may have horribly failed women, offspring, and God, we too can become one after God's own heart by accepting responsibly, repenting, and then pivoting to position ourselves on God's side of the battlefield!

The story of David also provides a powerful model of repentance. Psalms 51 is David's Psalm of repentance and forgiveness. It reads as follows: Psalm 51:1-17 *"For the director of music. A psalm of David. When the prophet Nathan came to him after David had committed adultery with Bathsheba.* 1 Have mercy on me, O God, according to your unfailing love; according to your great compassion blot out my transgressions. 2 Wash away all my iniquity and cleanse me from my sin. 3 For I know my transgressions, and my sin is always before me. 4 Against you, you only, have I sinned and done what is evil in your sight; so you are right in your verdict and justified when you judge. 5 Surely, I was sinful at birth, sinful from the time my mother conceived me. 6 Yet you desired faithfulness even in the womb; you taught me wisdom in that secret place. 7 Cleanse me with hyssop, and I will be clean; wash me, and I will be whiter than snow. 8 Let me hear joy and gladness; let the bones you have crushed rejoice. 9 Hide your face from my sins and blot out all my iniquity. 10 Create in me a pure heart, O God, and renew a steadfast spirit within me. 11 Do not cast me from your presence or take your Holy Spirit from me. 12 Restore to me the joy of your salvation and grant me a willing spirit, to sustain me. 13 Then I will teach transgressors your ways so that sinners will turn back to you. 14 Deliver me from the guilt of bloodshed, O God, you who are God my Savior, and my tongue will sing of your righteousness. 15 Open my lips, Lord, and my mouth will declare your praise. 16 You do not delight in sacrifice, or I would bring it; you do not take pleasure in burnt offerings. 17 My sacrifice, O God, is[b] a broken spirit; a broken and contrite heart you, God, will not despise."

This Psalm sheds light on why King David is heralded as "a man after God's own heart." We see David's plea for mercy, his sincere desire to have all transgressions washed away, a desire for a pure heart, and renewed Spirit, and we see his broken and contrite heart that leads to repentance. Since we, like David, have all failed miserably in myriad ways, it is refreshing to know we can still be deemed as people who lived as if we were "after God's own heart" (even after countless failures).

David came in contact with "base" frailties of his hedonistic nature and saw he needed help in the depths of his soul. At that moment, David "surrendered." This meant he came to the end of himself and wanted only what God (in His divine grace and mercies) wanted to give him gong forward. God knew David's heart was broken and repentant and immediately began to deliver and restore him, and perpetually honors him as a model for those seeking after His heart. It all began with David's surrender. In the context of our foe's myriad tactics, many will now realize their (unwitting) folly and come to the end of themselves in surrender to God; they'll relinquish insatiable rage, anger, frustration, and the seething demand for recompense based on "war on women," "racism," "reparations," and other known satanic distractions. This is the key to the revival of the soul in America, and I pray this is inevitable!

Surrendering to God may prove difficult for some, but it is necessary. The capacity to observe and confront the base nature lodged in the depths of our soul prompts the need to be forgiven for our (individual) malignant acts, but it doesn't stop there. It's coupled with a need to extend forgiveness to others who may have acted untoward us. God designed the act of forgiveness as a co- ontogenic mechanism for healing; when appropriately applied, it's a two-way concurrent action (focused both inward and outward) that "breaks" you and "re-makes" you at the same time. The Bible confirms that Jesus modeled co-ontogenic aspects of forgiveness in "Lords Prayer." Matthew 6:12 says, "…and forgive us our sins, as we have forgiven those who sin against us." In Matthew 6:14, Jesus says further, "If you forgive those who sin against you, your heavenly Father will forgive you." It cannot be understated; the complete work of forgiveness is to be received inwardly (personal) and extended outwardly (toward others) in a two-way co- ontogenic modality. God forgives humanity for transgressions, and He desires humanity to extend forgiveness to one another. In both instances, God pushes humanity to "let go"(surrender). He desires humankind to come to Him when we come to the "end of ourselves" with a broken and contrite heart. Additionally, God's freeing works are fully realized when humanity learns to forgive others to the extent it no longer suffers and holds- fast to contempt toward others based on feelings of oppression, victimization, and being burdened by endless thoughts of injustice. Forgiveness, as modeled by David, provides a model for real healing from the past, while confirming healing, restoration, and freedom to move forward.

As a distinction, forgiveness is an idea that seems so simple, its almost cliché. While it may seem conceptually simplistic, entrenched mindsets encased in strongholds of bitterness and resentment prevent the ability to experience freedom and restoration God provides. The reason is, while asking God to forgive individual sins, many still hold some level of animus (willful unforgiveness) toward others, and this is not freeing; its bondage! Bondage always reproduces. Bondage (in and of itself) has a tendency to produce more bondage, which then cascades to the point it is embraced as a blanket. Our foe uses blankets of pride, arrogance and un-forgiveness, and insatiable indignation as bondage, so most never experience true freedom. God's forgiveness, exemplified via David, is the only way to escape cycles of bondage.

...many who seem to always find ways to assert they're aggrieved, "put upon," victimized, oppressed, racially discriminated against and etc., will continue to actually fight for satan and against women because battling on the side of unforgiveness provides a blanket and "salve" for ever-insatiable "trigger-mongers."

The significance of forgiveness (and likewise unforgiveness) is due to its huge implications for our foe as he battles against God and humanity. Our foe uses unforgiveness to tether and enslave soldiers to his side of the battle against God and humanity. Since unforgiveness seeps to the soul, it's used to embolden arrogantly; satan encourages pride and arrogance to dismiss any solutions that could lead to freedom and restoration. To be sure, even with Biblical facts in this book about the "root," "fruit," and determined foe waging a cosmic war against God (via women and offspring), many who seem to always find ways to assert they're aggrieved, "put upon," victimized, oppressed, racially discriminated against and etc., will continue to actually fight for satan and against women because battling on the side of unforgiveness provides a blanket and "salve" for ever-insatiable "trigger-mongers."

In summary, God's model of forgiveness is designed as an example to us for-giving to others. Extending forgiveness for racism, assaults, molestations, disappointments, and any number of maltreatments are difficult, but they are necessary. As stated, forgiveness not only puts us in "right standing" with God, it delivers us from undue suffering and resentments, thus setting us free. If forgiveness can be fully perceived and appreciated as a strategic pivot point that changes our direction and position on the cosmic battlefield, it will be more easily relied upon to bring forth healing, restoration, and freedom of the soul. God is pleased to heal and deliver those who offer this level of surrender. Like David, due to our own surrender, brokenness, and contrition, perhaps there will be memorials in the heavens that will tout we (individually) are men and women "after God's own heart"....

Closing Argument

The fact that everyone is born into sin, possess a sin nature, and produce acts accordingly, confirm everyone needs to arrive at a point of repentance and be forgiven. If we are committed to fighting on God's side of the cosmic battlefield, repentance and subsequent forgiveness (God's forgiveness toward us, and our forgiveness toward others) are not optional; they are mandatory! David modeled that irrespective of the depths of personal sin, God can and will forgive! He also modeled a sincere, broken, and contrite heart tender towards God is the posture for repentance that God honors and views as our pursuit "after His own heart." When we meet in eternity, will we find God has memorialized our pursuit of His own heart?

CHAPTER 14

HOLY WHOLLY WHOLE ARMOR: WEAPONS FOR WAGING WAR & WINNING BATTLES

Opening Statement

"The battle" is actually not ours; it's the Lords! This requires, however, that we get out of His way so He can do His mighty works while waging the battle against our foe. How do we get out of God's way? We prepare ourselves by accepting His Son, then get wisdom and understanding of the cosmic battle and consequences, position ourselves on His side of battlefield, yield "our members" to Him, so He can use us as "vessels" to do great works, and wholly submit to His Lordship! In the end, God wins battles by divine inspiration working through us! In all, our foe's enmity is defeated, and God wins the war!

God honors, cherishes, and values women so much that He entrusted woman (solely) to incubate and deliver His most precious gift to the world, His Son. Jesus, the Son of God, through His commitment to love all, and heal and deliver, permanently shifts the trajectory of the cosmic battlefield.

Through being born into this realm, Jesus was our "older Brother" and perfect example. He was tempted on all sides as we all are, yet He overcame all temptations and sin; He was sinless! After conquering all temptations, death, hell, and the grave, He was given all power (in the heavens and earth) and adroitly decimated our eternal foe. Now, the same power that Jesus took back from our foe extends to all humanity! We access this power by simply acknowledging Jesus (His birth, death on the cross, and resurrection power), repenting, and then accepting His forgiveness. After these simple acts of contrition in deference to God's Kingdom authority, we become equipped to fight on god's side in the cosmic battle…with the fullness of the power and authority extended through our Savior Jesus. Jesus is the divine "equalizer" who forever abolished the enmity that precipitated the war from the beginning.

Enmity is defined as hostility, hatred, and war. As repeatedly confirmed, satan's enmity (war) against God and humanity is the dividing line that Jesus came to destroy; Jesus demolishes all enmity, hostilities, and hatred via the cross. Ephesians 2:14-16 (NIV) confirms, "14 For he himself is our peace, who has made the two groups one and has destroyed the barrier, the dividing wall of hostility, 15 by setting aside in his flesh the law with its commands and regulations. His purpose was to create in himself one new humanity … thus making peace, 16 and in one body to reconcile both of them (Jew and Gentile) to God through the cross, by which he put to death their hostility.[36]

Offspring that will crush the head of the serpent (noted in Genesis 3:15) points directly to Jesus. While all humanity is reflective of offspring from women, Jesus is the "seed" specifically noted that inevitably crushes the serpent. Further, through His triumph over death, hell and grave, all others will gain power and authority to do the same. He came to change the battlefield trajectory from defeatist to victorious by permanently shifting all aspects of the cosmic battlefield toward God. Where our foe stridently works to divide humanity based on nefarious factors like race, gender, wealth, class, identity politics and etc., Jesus came to wholly unify humanity into one supreme fighting force battling on God's side of the cosmic battlefield. Jesus alone reconciles all into one unified body and fighting force; through Him, all hostility and enmity are destroyed, allowing humanity to triumph over any/all strongholds and addictions our foe uses to tether to his side of the battlefield. Acceptance of Jesus' power

---

[36] *New International Version (NIV) Holy Bible, New International Version®, NIV® Copyright ©1973, 1978, 1984, 2011 by Biblica, Inc.® Used by*

and authority put individuals in direct alignment with God's Kingdom. In His Kingdom, the army of God is groomed, matured, and equipped (with Kingdom armor) to fight our foe.

Jesus is not only Savior and Lord, He is the lead warrior and "equipper" on the cosmic battlefield. He fully equips for the battle against our foe. As with any battle, the key to waging war and winning requires proper equipment and tools. While our foe uses negative emotions like angst, unforgiveness, and pride as a way to generate zeal for soldiers on his side of battlefield, God equips His soldiers with a "full armor of God"; this armor has offensive and defensive purposes and is mandatory for each participant on God's side of the battlefield.

Ephesians 6:10-17 (GNT) confirms, "Finally, build up your strength in union with the Lord and by means of his mighty power. [11] Put on all the armor that God gives you so that you will be able to stand up against the Devil's evil tricks. [12] For we are not fighting against human beings but against the wicked spiritual forces in the heavenly world, the rulers, authorities, and cosmic powers of this dark age. [13] So put on God's armor now! Then when the evil day comes, you will be able to resist the enemy's attacks; and after fighting to the end, you will still hold your ground. [14] So stand ready, with truth as a belt tight around your waist, with righteousness as your breastplate, [15] and as your shoes the readiness to announce the Good News of peace. [16] At all times carry faith as a shield; for with it, you will be able to put out all the burning arrows shot by the Evil One. [17] And accept salvation as a helmet, and the word of God as the sword which the Spirit gives you." These verses are prescient to the extent they confirm our foe and his minions as wicked spiritual forces, but though we are human, they can be effectively fought with the armor of God.

Wielding the armor of God provides us all we need to win the cosmic battle being waged in this realm. While all pieces of armor are necessary, especially noteworthy is the sword of the Spirit (which is the Word of God) that's to be forcefully thrust forth by purposeful, targeted and precise rebuttals to our enemy's schemes to undermine our resolve. Likewise, the shield of Faith is waved with force, confidence, and full expectation to eliminate "fiery darts" (all our foe's tricks, lies and schemes). Finally, as our foe continues to press forward with attacks, the helmet of salvation keeps our minds steady, the breastplate keeps our heart righteous and ready, and the binds on our waist (truth) and feet (peace) allow us to endure and extend success in the battle while reclaiming enemy territory! In practical terms, Jesus has fully equipped us with the armor of God so we can make the most positive difference in the arenas where our foe is most actively engaged; this means we are fully equipped to take him on and engage civically, culturally, and societally.

One of the most effective ways to solder on God's side of the battlefield is taking a definitive stand! When God's soldiers take a definitive stand for God (and by extension women and offspring), our foe loses territory. When Churches/Clergy take a stand to affirm God's primacy for the sanctity of human life (from conception to birth, to nurturing, to natural death), our foe retreats. When the Supreme Court and other justices stand for women and offspring by affirming the significance of the sanctity of human life as Constitutional (via affirmative statements in Declaration of Independence and the Constitution), the territory of our foe shrinks. When the President of the U.S. affirms the sanctity of human life as important and significant, then nominate court judges that affirm the same, our foe is decimated. When scientists continue to dutifully affirm "life" begins at conception, our foe is deflated. When those committed to God's battlefield put on the full armor of God while participating socially, culturally, and especially civically (to the extent, we take a stand consistent with only supporting public representatives who wholly support the sanctity of women and offspring), satan is defeated! The point is, since the cosmic battle revolves around our foe targeting and maligning women and respective offspring, we can shift and change trajectories of the battlefield by taking a stand consistent with the support of women and offspring in all life domains.

It so happens that we (in America) have a divine blessing that gives the ability to take a stand by merely voting. This simple act confirms who we are, what we believe, and our zeal for change. If we don't like what's happening in our country, we can change it with our vote. Voting also confirms the side of the cosmic battlefield one stands on, as it confirms personal ideology, theology (or lack thereof), and a Biblical stance/beliefs (or not)! If people still zealously vote and support those (individuals or

organizations) who stridently undermine God via undermining His wil
upholding the sanctity of life, they're social activists/revolutionaries
committed to our foe. If people still strictly vote with Political Parties
who stand antithetical to God's side of the battlefield, they confirm
they're strident activists complicit with pinning for our foe. Politica
Parties that encourage "shout your abortion," and encourage abortion as
a noble and honorable cause, are committed to demonic folly and wholly
undeserving of receiving a vote from people committed to women and
offspring (God's side of the cosmic battlefield). Today's Democrat Party
is a good example of a political Party stridently encouraging what is now
untenable. A Politico article titled "If You're a pro- life Democrat ..
You Know You're Standing Alone"[37] confirms the National Committee
Chairman of Democrat Party Tom Perez publicly proclaimed that "every
Democrat" should support abortion rights. The article details Perez's
fervent commitment to assert abortion as a litmus test for all Democrats
(especially those running for office).

In contrast to prevailing mindsets of Progressive Democrats, Dr. Rav
Zacharias says this about the sanctity of life, "There are only two options
either go to God on His terms and find our perfect peace in His acceptance
of us, or play God with self-defining morality and kill--becoming as a resul
restless wanderers, ever running from the voice of our brothers' blood tha
cries out from the ground. At its core life is sacred and of inestimable
value, whether it is life of a child in the fresh blossom of childhood, o
the life of an elderly recluse. Both have one thing in common: they are
made in the image of God. We may try intellectual duplicity to rearrange
the furniture of life and define it only in material terms, but each time
we sit back and read of genocide or human trafficking, we shift and turn
with revulsion, realizing that there is no harmony in the secular "decor,"
for the cry within the sacred cannot be suppressed. That is the reason
we scream forth *Why?* at the headlines: we cannot silence the still, smal
voice inside that speaks of the intrinsic sanctity of life and that it ough
not be violated."[38]

[37] Politico JENNIFER HABERKORN, "If You're a pro-life Democrat You Know
[38] Zondervan, Ravi Zacharias, The Logic of God 2019. Chapt. 29- Rearranging the
furniture

Our vote provides one of our most important "checks" on our foe's' myriad schemes to undermine and decimate humanity. The ability to vote is surely a blessing for all Americans. When you compare our ability to vote with other large countries like China (where people haven't been able to have their vote count in almost 100 years), Russia's rigged voting system(s), and India's sporadic democratic voting, we can see Americans are truly blessed to be able to have direct impact and change direction of our government via the cherished function of casting a simple vote. In addition to effecting society via striving to be living epistles and testimonies, asserting our morals and values, and becoming people who live "beyond reproach" in our respective communities, voting is of at least equal importance. Our vote is representative of cumulative power that (when cast) acts as a catalyst to intervening in current socio/cultural trajectory. It is one of the more powerful ways to strategically impacting the battle on God's side of the cosmic battlefield. If people vote en masse for God's side, the change will be immediate, and our foe will lose insurmountable portions of the cosmic territory. If we vote for satan's side (the side targeting women and offspring for destruction) or don't vote at all, our foe will continue his brazen assaults and unfettered destruction. It is important to remember, since everyone is already enlisted on one side of the battlefield or the other, everyone is voting by default (whether affirmatively casting a vote or not, your vote is counted). While "non-voters" may see themselves as "apolitical" and "above the fray, " their "non-vote" is actually a vote for the current trajectory! If voters want satan to continue the targeted assault of women and offspring, their non- vote counts to assure the current trajectory continues. If, however, voters would like to intervene and see things change, a vote must be cast; fervent prayer and consistently casting votes are the only ways to effectively intervene and disrupt current socio/cultural trajectory.

If someone is committed to helping change culture and society, one of the worst things you can do is not to vote. Ironically the power of the vote in America is taken for granted. To be sure, most who purport to stand with and for God's side, don't vote. Just as when Adam and Eve ceded their power and authority to satan in the garden (through rebellion), people who don't vote cede their power and authority (after its regained via acceptance of Jesus) to our foe through "complicit rebellion." In

THE WAR ON WOMEN

other words, most know culture and society are not trending toward God, yet through dereliction to vote, they create a vacuum that actually enshrines schemes and machinations that increase trending toward our foe. "America has reached its spiritual kairos, the culmination of the last two or three generations of Christian indolence and disregard to secular onslaught and incursion. Allowing those in rebellion against God not only to be elected to office but to seize the levers of control over America's cultural mountains of influence, such indifference is lethal. Even so, the Church remains dormant. In off-year elections - 2018, 2014, 2010 - 12%-15% of Christians were voting. In other words, 85%-88% of Christians abstained from their civic responsibility. Incredibly, people are mystified how and why America, after 350 years, lost its Judeo- Christian heritage and Biblically-based culture. Looking back through America's history, we can be certain that the Founders would neither have retreated from social and political involvement in the public square nor have submitted to any effort to dechristianize America's civil government, law, and public life. Contemporary Christians, as a whole, have withdrawn from the public square, and spiritual wisdom no longer prompts and propels 'social action, education, intellectual pursuits, the shaping of culture, and political thought and action."[39]

Having yielded to "the unaided reason of man [whose arrogant mentality has placed him or herself] above the authority of the Scriptures, denied the inspiration and infallibility of the Bible, renounced the reality of Original Sin, rejected the Trinity - the divinity of Jesus Christ and the Holy Spirit - and waged war upon Biblical orthodoxy," America has accordingly surrendered to "state-controlled education and civil government coercion to 'reform' man and society along man-centered lines." So concluded Archie P. Jones in his Foreword to the new edition of Christian Life and Character of the Civil Institutions of the United States [1864]. He continued by saying:

> *"Romans 13 and the Bible as a whole make so clear that civil government is not neutral among religions and philosophies of men but instead a ministry of the sovereign God who created and*

---

[39]   *Dr, Ravi Zacharias, The Logic of God, Zondervan 2019*

*rules His Universe and world, and works out His eternal plan
and holy will in history. Our forefathers in faith did not retreat
from involvement in society and politics. They did not turn civil
government, the making, enforcement, and adjudication of laws,
over to Satan and those who serve him. They did not surrender
the ministry of civil government to those who are in rebellion
against God. Instead, they sought to base civil government and
law upon truth."*

In conjunction with living in God's Kingdom, being clothed in the
whole armor of God, and being an exemplary citizen in the community,
the single act of voting is one the best strategically significant offensive
weapons to be used in this realm in order to thwart satan's machination
and schemes destined to malign women and offspring. When all who love
God take a definitive stand and vote in alignment with God's side of the
battlefield, America will experience revival, renewal, and restoration.

There are still huge obstacles with seeing the majority of society
becoming aligned with God's side of the battlefield. One of the biggest
obstacles is unconstrained personal pride, as pride always rejects Lordship.
Fundamental to accepting Jesus is accepting Him as Savior and Lord.
Most are keen on the "Savior" aspect of Jesus, but when it comes to living
under the Lordship of Christ, intense internal battles with personal pride
and traditions prevent the total transformation (and "death to self") God
desires. Lack of full embrace of Christ's Lordship is quite apparent when
observing the numbers of "Christians'" who have a tremendous zeal for
Political affiliations and social movements antithetical to God's Word. If
indeed we only went to the ballot box strictly motivated by Lordship of
Christ, determined to only support individuals and entities more closely
aligned with the Bible (notably God's side of the battlefield), we would have
significantly different results. Lordship would mandate voting and dictate
how to vote, and in turn, release any personal attachment to political Parties
and individuals out of the equation. In the end, we would see a notable
change in the socio/cultural trajectory, and our foe will experience huge
territorial losses. Regrettably, it seems many "Christians" defiantly (albeit
perhaps unwittingly) reject the Lordship of Christ and continue to pridefully
assert they don't have to vote, and/or "can- never" and "will-never" vote

for certain Parties or people even if those entities demonstrate a definitive commitment to God's side of the battlefield (demonstrable undergirding of women and offspring by upholding God's standards for "sanctity of human life"); this is a primary example of defiant rejection of Lordship! The vote is another area that confirms our foe has been masterful at creating entrenched mindsets driven purely by emotion, smitten with foolery, and devoid of common sense and rationality. It's these mindsets that have been determining outcomes of our vote (and the ensuing socio/cultural chaos); henceforth, its time for the 75% of Christians tacitly supporting satan's battlefield (due to their "non- votes") to take a definitive stand for God and vote finally!

It cannot be overstated that your side of the battlefield is confirmed by your personal ideology, personal theology, Biblical stance/beliefs, and your vote! Again, your vote (whether actively voting or passively voting) unmistakably and inextricably confirms the battlefield you're fighting on. That said, intense disagreements between and amongst one another actually have little to do with Political Parties or die-hard support (or rejection) of individuals in power; most of what separates us is quite trivial. Race, Political Party, gender, "wealth," social status, "Class," and myriad others characteristics are our foe's tactics at distracting humanity via "trivial pursuits!" While they seem to carry real weight, they are ostensibly designed to keep humanity emotionally charged with caricatures that veil the cosmic battle. Devoid of real meaning and purpose (compared to the cosmic battle that rages), their singular purpose is separate society into easily managed factions. Our foe purposefully uses factions to generate angst, and uses identity politics to drive a wedge between individuals. After wholly distracted, he distracts and dissuades from taking affirmative actions for God's side of the battle; satan consistently uses mind-numbing sophomoric distractions to emotionally-charge the masses toward entrenched animus, chaos and disunity, and (regrettably) this is what has had the biggest impact on our vote! While some want to see society/culture change direction but view the act of not voting as a noble and (somehow) virtuous, our foe relishes in this mindset for his gain. Satan gains strength and his side of the battlefield, and it expands when people don't vote. If people desire a change in trajectory in culture/society, yet they chose not to vote, their act (not voting) is wholly ignoble and demonstrably connotes the lack of embrace of Lordship. God sent His Son as our perfect example, and He was wholly engaged in all domains of life (social/cultural/religious/education/government/family and etc.). Again, intense commitment to Lordship is the key, and we must recommit to it.

There are many impediments that prevent us from being able to clearly perceive how we should civically engage in support of righteousness and justice. In addition to grotesque reprobation's spread via Liberation Theology and other antithetical teachings, sanctimonious moralizers like the Christianity Today publication, "theologian" Jim Wallis, and social activists like Father Pfleger have only helped our foe as he wages war on women and offspring; their help toward our foe comes from actively encouraging voters to support people, organizations and Parties standing on our foe's side of battlefield! They seem completely oblivious to the cosmic battle and, therefore, sanctimoniously smear all those who dissent from their point of view. The good news going forward is, we no longer have to endure partisan diatribes and feigned moral outrages from others about how we should respond to those who don't seem to comport with "Christian perfection." We now have full capacity to make a simple and straight forward assessment about who deserves our endorsement and support via their stance for or against satan's war on women. If they support irreconcilable "intersections" that actually hurt women and annihilate children, they are soldiers for our foe. If not, they're simpatico with God. The point is, with a focus on satan's war against women and offspring and a personal commitment to stand and battle on God's side of the cosmic battlefield, all oblique and sophomoric considerations that currently dominate civic engagement like Political Parties, race, wealth and etc., should go away. At this time in history, there's a tremendous need to reject our eternal foe's tactics and schemes, and wholly focus on becoming Christians "surrendered" unto the Holy Lordship of Christ.

Philosopher and theologian, GK Chesterton, said, The Christian ideal has not been tried and found wanting. It has been found difficult; and left untried"[40] If Christians don't intervene with consistent voting on and for God's side of the battlefield, current trajectory dictates, we will lose the ability to vote at all. Socialism/Marxism is now acceptable,

---

[40] *American Minute Dec 5 2019, Bill Federer Pastors in Politics during Revolution: Hugh Williamson & other preachers*

iron-fisted authoritarian "big government" is now becoming acceptable, fascist protests are now in vogue, restrictions on "speech" are now acceptable, and the entire Bill Of Rights seems "up for grabs." America is rapidly approaching the precipice of an abyss (of sorts); once it eclipses that precipice, the sheer inertia will make it impossible to turn back. A signatory to the U.S. Constitution, Dr. Hugh Williamson stated (while on his deathbed), "The most important thing is to bring people to Christ; the second most important thing is to preserve the freedom to do the most important thing!" Church leaders not involved in preserving the freedom to preach the Gospel are effectively admitting they really do not believe preaching the Gospel is that important."[41]

What more is there? The Church has been silent on too many things that supremely matter to God. Satan wages war against women and offspring as a proxy to exact devastation as an affront to God, yet God's children are mostly asleep. But due to its vast implications, this war has primacy in God's view. It started in the garden and has been raging ever since. This is the battle for all of humanity, but too often, humanity seems to unwittingly accommodate it's arch-enemy and foe (by remaining silent and therefore complicit), instead of resolute in opposition to him. German theologian and Pastor Dietrich Bonhoeffer is quoted as saying, "Silence in the face of evil is itself evil: God will not hold us guiltless. Not to speak is to speak. Not to act is to act." As the Church of Christ, under Lordship of Christ, we stand for Christ, by standing and fighting on God's side of the battlefield.

Which side are YOU on?

Concluding Argument

Self-deception is a horrible taskmaster. Our foe uses this brand of deception to overrule personal religious convictions, logic, reason, and rationality in order to keep Christians silent and complicit with his schemes to undermine women and offspring in his war. The result has been devastating! Most Christians are not voting, and therefore there's minimal Godly "check" on

[41] *American Minute Dec 5 2019, Bill Federer Pastors in Politics during Revolution: Hugh Williamson & other preachers*

124

Americas Representative Government; this means most people in power are secular humanists wholly committed to our foe's battlefield. Sadly, many desire to see a change in socio/cultural trajectory, but decline to vote. Christians have been unwittingly tethered to our foe's battlefield by simply being agnostic to the need to vote, and as a result, our enemy has gained significant battleground territory in his war against God and humanity. Ironically, many may put on the whole armor of God, they may live appropriate to religious convictions, but due to their "non-vote," they continually enshrine and embolden satan's side of the battlefield. Self-deception, pride, and lack of Lordship (all symptomatic of focus on "self") are the culprits and must be necessarily sacrificed "at the Cross"....

CHAPTER 15

CONCLUSION

The Verdict

It's been confirmed that since the beginning, humanity has been
overwhelmed by satan's onslaught of diabolical schemes in
his war with God; by proxy, he's been waging a relentless war
against women and offspring in order to undermine God and
humanity. As a result of satan's tactics, women and babies are
the most helpless, maligned, and harassed demographics on
the planet. If we were to respond to satan's war against them in
ways that are kind and truly compassionate, we would reject our
foe's schemes (like pornography, sex/slavery/prostitution, racist/
infanticide of Planned Parenthood, and all other noted factions)
and offer God's loving-kindness and compassion found in Jesus!
He (alone) destroys enmity, and all nuances and structures of
satan's war…The verdict is in! How will you respond?

This book meandered through many fundamental facts (and even
tertiary aspects) of satan's war on women. What are we to conclude? The
only question that requires a definitive answer is, "Which side are you on?"

An analogy using a tree with "roots" and "fruit" provided the ability to
observe better our foe's cause, tactics, and strategies used to fight against
God and humanity. If the root and fruit were confirmed, "What of the tree?"
What is the actual tree representative of? For the purposes of this book,

consider the tree as analogous to the soul. It was posited upfront that the arena of the soul (where we hold preexisting notions and heartfelt beliefs about prevailing nomenclature surrounding "the war on women") would be challenged, and throughout this book, we journeyed to the depths of soul (where the mind, will and emotions reside) so appropriate "pruning," or "replanting" and/or necessary amount of "re- nourishing" can take place to repair it (if necessary). As with any planting/pruning cycle, results may be immediately noticeable but may take some time before the "tree" fully flourishes anew. Likewise, our soul may immediately begin to change, but it may take some time to fully ingest then abundantly flourish from new revelations presented in this book. While women (collectively) represent the battlefield for our foe's war, the arena of the soul is the battlefield each individual must make decisions and take action (to help or hinder) the war on women; the trajectory of satan's war hinges on this vital inflection point. Dr Ravi Zacharias confirms, "The problem of evil has ultimately one source: it is the resistance of God's holiness that enshrouds all of creation. And there is ultimately only one hope for life: that is through the glorious display of God at work within the human soul. That transformation tenderizes the heart to become part of the solution and not part of the problem. Such transformation begins at the foot of the cross."

When it comes to intense battles (like the one now presented in the realm of the soul) words of Founding Father, philosopher, political theorist, and "father of the American Revolution," Thomas Paine seems especially poignant. In his writing of "Common Sense" and "The American Crisis," Paine's proclamations are prescient and can be directly relevant to current struggles in America. One of Paine's famous quotes is, "These are the times that try men's *souls*...." Indeed, our souls are tried and will be continuously tested by new revelations of our foe's war. Hopefully, your soul has already begun to adapt to a new way of thinking and behaving about satan's war on women. Nevertheless, Paine provides great additional context to ponder as you prepare to fight for God on behalf of women and offspring.

While he sparked divine prudence and confidence in the merits of fighting America's Revolutionary War, Paine also characterized the war in terms of good vs. evil. His wisdom (especially in the context of good vs. evil) transcends America's revolutionary period also to encompass the war on women we fight against today. Here are some of Paine's prescient quotes that seem directly relevant to the battle we face today: "It matters not where you live, or what rank of life you hold, the evil ... will reach you ...The blood of his children will curse his cowardice, who shrinks back at a time when a little might have saved the whole ... I love the man that can smile in trouble, that can gather strength from distress, and grow brave by reflection. 'Tis the business of little minds to shrink; but he whose heart is firm, and whose conscience approves his conduct, will pursue his principles unto death ..." "There are persons, too, who see not the full extent of the evil which threatens them; they solace themselves with hopes that the enemy if he succeeds, will be merciful. "It is the madness of folly, to expect mercy from those who have refused to do justice; and even mercy, where conquest is the object, is only a trick of war; the cunning of the fox is as murderous as the violence of the wolf, and we ought to guard equally against both." "Let them call me rebel ... I feel no concern from it... but I should suffer the misery of devils, were I to make a whore of my soul by swearing allegiance to one whose character is that of a sottish, stupid, stubborn, worthless, brutish man. I conceive likewise a horrid idea in receiving mercy from a being, who at the last day shall be shrieking to the rocks and mountains to cover him, and fleeing with terror from the orphan, the widow, and the slain of America." I have no doubt Thomas Paine was divinely inspired to have written the words that are timeless and transcend the centuries. While we will fight against our eternal foe, our preexisting mindsets, and our very soul, the fight can be eased if overlaid and characterized in the prescient and prophetic prose Paine proffered.

Our commitment to fighting on God's side of the battlefield requires extreme resolve. Our resolve should be unwavering since we have uncovered that there is a definitive war on women that satan began at the beginning of humanity. We uncovered that due to God's glory placed on them and their responsibility to birth and nurture humanity, women are the primary targets of our foe's schemes to undermine God and humanity. We uncovered that due to God's personal handiwork, eternal destiny, and the designation of "image-bearers," offspring (babies/children) are also primary targets in satan's war. To that end, we uncovered satan evolved ancient traditions to use of women in salacious forms of idol worship and encouraged child sacrifice as "progressive" and "noble" for "the enlightened." In this, our foe undermined God and humanity to the extent women and children were easily viewed as utilitarian "objects" as opposed to being viewed as cherished vessels of God's glory.

As time passed, our foe moved from women wholly exploiting themselves using anatomical objects during ancient rituals, to women wholly embracing exploitation of themselves via anatomically explicit costumes during public marches. At the same time, he moved from using ancient practices of incinerating living children as sacrifices on burning alters to now using racial animus as a way to spur acceleration and momentum in the elimination of babies before, during, and after birth (especially Black babies).

In order to obscure and shroud his definitive war on women, our foe used social movements as accelerants and "change agents" to dramatically shift perceptions about acceptable social/cultural norms; with these movements as "fronts" to his war, satan has been able to wholly decimate and undermine women and offspring while under a veil of relative obscurity. His cunning and deceptions have led "even the elect" astray (theologians, Clergy, academics, politicians, media, and etc.). In the end, God's "remnant" are needed to be the "check" on our foe's ability to continue to capture territory via his battleground assault on women (and offspring).

God foreknew humanity would arrive at this point in satan's the war on women and delivered "fresh wind" of revelation on Genesis 3:15 to help us perceive the battle as it has been raging for millennia. Actually, the Bible's last book, the transcendental book of Revelation (transcendental because the book of Revelation is revelatory of the past, present and future) confirms satan's war as it was conceived in the heavenlies before humankind was even created in the earthly realm. Since the book of Revelation carries significant weight and meaning, commentaries and interpretation run the gamut. But in summary, Revelation the 12th Chapter confirms, lucifer (dragon) was in heavens and he and his followers were cast out and relegated to earthly realm. It confirms satan pursued the woman because he knew should would ultimately give birth to the

THE WAR ON WOMEN

Savior. Further, it confirms that because he knew the women would be the conduit for humanity and the Savior would culminate in its redemption, he pursued women and "waged war against her and her offspring!" In the end, it also confirms that God's Son (Jesus/Yeshua) destroyed our foe's enmity against humankind and delivered all power and authority back to God's remnant. With renewed power and authority, the children of God can wage war against our defeated foe and win!

We can now begin changing the trajectory of the battlefield since the actual war on women has been confirmed, the foe (satan) identified, and tactics and strategies for socio/cultural change (intersectional social revolutionary movements) have been unveiled. By wielding the whole armor of God, fully representing God and His Kingdom by living exemplary lives, and by taking a simple quite-practical step of voting in every election (for individuals and/or policies that undergird women and offspring according to dictates of the cosmic battle), we can appropriately intervene and take back battleground and territory while standing and fighting on God's side of the battlefield. God has ordained His children would be mightily used in this hour to finally stomp on the head of the serpent and thwart his continued unfettered assault on God and humanity.

In consideration of Chapter 7, "<u>If I Were The Devil</u>," here are some additional devilish characterizations to append:

If I were the devil, I would continue to veil mankind's hearts and minds to Planned Parenthood's continued, persistent and systemic structures of racism designed to utterly eliminate Black and Brown populations

If I were the devil, I would doggedly blind readers to the truths and facts presented in this book and veil their memory in order to neutralize and trivialize any change in mindset or personal impact

If I were the devil, I would force readers to holdfast to "their truth" (ideological strongholds) and arcanely reject and dismiss this reading as "right-wing," "conspiratorial," "racist" delusions

If I were the devil, I would use "theologians" to encourage others to somehow characterize this book as esoteric machinations that must be rejected. This will prevent readers from embracing its Biblically accurate depictions of my war on women and the unleashing of Spiritual warfare

If I were the devil, I'd whisper to all readers, "How, and/or whether you vote are decisions God has no interest in (or thoughts about)." I'd urge, "Just keep doing what you're doing"...

If I were the devil, I'd encourage readers to completely dismiss the truths about the power of prayer, repentance and forgiveness! These weapons utterly destroy my schemes and strategies that continue to enslave hearts, minds and subsequent actions of mankind. As humanity's fundamental foe, these weapons must be undermined!

The realm of the soul is where the transition begins from being easily triggered, gripped and swept into emotion-driven hateful rage about the plight of women, to the point of being gripped and swept into wise understanding of God's side of the cosmic battlefield (and dutifully committing to fight *for* women and against all schemes of our foe). The foundation has been laid to help better comprehend the actual battle via a new way of observing, a new way of being engaged in the battle, a new way of serving women and offspring, and a new way of voting as a way to affirmatively take a stand for God and humanity. To be sure, this new understanding will take us well beyond "politics," political Parties, and mundane personal ideologies, and instead leads us to the heart of how to stand for righteousness and justice. It's binary, so irrespective of what we claim, our actions going forward will easily confirm which side we stand on and for whom we fight. If we stand with God and for women and offspring, we will assert the primacy and importance of the sanctity of life (and will vote for people and policies accordingly). If we don't take these actions, we are standing on the other battlefield and tacitly stand *against* women. Simple!

Here's the "light at the end of the tunnel," unwittingly supporting satan doesn't make you a Satanist. Unwittingly supporting abortions doesn't make you a racist abortionist. Unwittingly supporting community organizing doesn't make you a radical globalist anarchist. And unwittingly supporting Black Liberation Theology doesn't mean you're anti-Christ. But, wittingly supporting these going forward does confirm you are not actually fighting "*for women*" and fighting to help women; it means you are decidedly and willfully fighting *against women* (and offspring). Righteously fighting on God's side of the battlefield is the *ONLY* side of battle indicative of a commitment to stand for justice in support of women and children!

In the end, satan's war against God and humanity is eternal (never-ending); it's targeted to decimate women and offspring, and its binary. While all of humanity is automatically enlisted into the battle, every individual can decide which battlefield they will stand, battle, and fight on. In practical terms, individuals can choose continued embrace of our foe's adolescent and sophomoric schemes to divide humanity via gratuitous grievances over race, wealth/status, gender, religion, political Party (personal ideologies) and etc., but the only significant data point/ criteria going forward is "What battlefield are you fighting on?" If we adopt this data point as the lens that dictates our worldview (guiding our social and civil engagement) we can regain the capacity to unify in order to help our fractured schools, Churches, family, government and society (in general). It cannot be overstated, irrespective of how one chooses to justify their stance going forward, the fact remains, individuals can only stand on one side of the battle or the other; not both! Every individual is forced to decide whether to fight for satan's war *on* women or God's battle *for* women (empowering and undergirding women and offspring). Only YOU can confirm and dictate which battlefield you are aligned with and will assuredly fight on. Remember, our greatest enemy is not the enemy from without, but rather one from within. That said, irrespective of your words, and how you may attempt to reconcile the irreconcilable in order to continue to fight for the foe that hates and wants to decimate you and all of humanity, your actions confirm it all!

Which side of the battlefield are YOU on?

Made in the USA
Monee, IL
09 September 2021

76893444R00085